MAKING CHILDREN MIND
WITHOUT LOSING YOURS

If you're interested in bringing up children who are responsible, loving, and respectful to you and others—then this book can be a real help. With loving discipline you can teach your children to be accountable for their actions. More than that, you can give them a special gift they can use all of their lives: preparation and training for the realities of everyday living. And as a bonus you will find freedom from the "following them around all day to make sure they behave" syndrome. How does all this happen? Through a practical, commonsense approach that is based on using action, not words. It's called . . . Reality Discipline.

MAKING CHILDREN MIND

WITHOUT LOSING YOURS

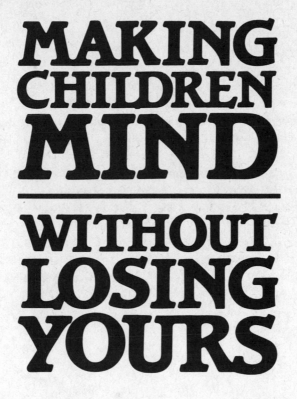

Dr. KEVIN LEMAN

Fleming H. Revell Company
Old Tappan, New Jersey

Scripture quotations identified KJV are from the King James Version of the Bible.

Scripture quotations identified TLB are from The Living Bible, copyright © 1971 by Tyndale House Publishers, Wheaton, IL. Used by permission.

Scripture quotations identified NIV are from the HOLY BIBLE: NEW INTERNATIONAL VERSION, Copyright © 1978 by the New York International Bible Society. Used by permission of Zondervan Bible Publishers.

Quotation from GOD, THE ROD, AND YOUR CHILD'S BOD by Larry Tomczak. Copyright © 1981, 1982, by Larry and Doris Tomczak, published by Fleming H. Revell Company. Used by permission.

Library of Congress Cataloging in Publication Data
Leman, Kevin.
    Making children mind without losing yours.
    1. Discipline of children.   2. Child rearing.
3. Parenting—Religious aspects—Christianity.   I. Title.
HQ770.4.L44   1984   649'.64   83-11233
ISBN 0-8007-1373-7

To Kristin Sarah Leman, our middle child and younger daughter, who endured many hand-me-downs and far fewer pictures in the family photo album. Your contagious smile, your sensitivity to others, and your love for God make me proud to be your daddy. I love you, Krissy. God bless you.

Contents

Foreword

Reality Discipline: Its Time Has Come!

As a psychologist and a parent with three children of my own, I'm enthused about this book because I believe Reality Discipline is an idea whose time has come. What is Reality Discipline? Reality Discipline is a consistent, decisive, and respectful way for parents to love and discipline their children. Now notice I said "discipline" and not "punish." And notice that I also said "love" and not "smother love" their children.

I'm as happy as anyone that we no longer live in the Dark Ages when children were supposed to be seen and not heard and heaven help them if they let out a peep. I'm also relieved to see that we no longer wallow in the overpermissiveness of the 1950s and '60s, which saw many parents being led astray by the people in my profession who told them that disciplining their children would inhibit their little psyches and cause all kinds of psychological havoc.

But the reason I think the time has come for Reality Discipline is that I see many families today who are groping between the two extremes I've just described. As a family therapist I talk to parents and their children every week. I also travel the length and breadth of the land to speak to groups of parents and teachers about child rearing, disci-

9

pline, and guidance. What I see and hear is that, in too many homes today, otherwise sophisticated and educated parents are still not sure they know the difference between discipline and punishment, between permissiveness and loving nurture. I believe that difference is clearly spelled out in a brief passage from the New Testament where the Apostle Paul writes:

> Children, obey your parents; this is the right thing to do because God has placed them in authority over you. Honor your father and mother. This is the first of God's Ten Commandments that ends with a promise. And this is the promise: that if you honor your father and mother, yours will be a long life, full of blessing. And now a word to you parents. Don't keep on scolding and nagging your children, making them angry and resentful. Rather, bring them up with the loving discipline the Lord himself approves, with suggestions and godly advice.
>
> Ephesians 6:1–4, TLB

The above Scripture passage is the basis for this book. The words that we are going to pay particular attention to are *obey, authority,* and *loving discipline.*

My goal is to give parents specific ways to use their authority correctly as they bring up obedient children with loving discipline. One of the astounding things that I see again and again today is that many children do not feel loved in their own homes. In a survey of twenty-two hundred teenagers from Christian homes across the United States, 79 percent claimed they felt a lack of love at home. This startling figure was reported by Craig Massey, personality and radio family counselor who conducted the survey. In order for discipline to work, the first thing that must happen is that the child must feel genuinely loved. The key to Reality Discipline lies in the answers to questions like these:

How do I love my children?

How do I respect my children?

How do I hold my children accountable?

How do I get my children to do what I, the parent, think they ought to do, without resorting to physical or verbal violence?

What about spanking? Is it necessary? How much? How often?

At this point, you may be trying to place me on some kind of scale. How firm do I believe a parent should be? I believe that spanking has a place, but in most cases it should not take first place. At the same time, I am a firm believer that when we discipline children, their psyches are not in danger. The white-glove technique went out with the early excesses of Dr. Spock.

Reality Discipline uses guidance and *action-oriented* techniques. Action-oriented discipline is based on the reality that there are times—sometimes several per day—when you have to pull the rug out and let the little "buzzards" tumble. I don't mean that literally, of course, but when I talk about pulling the rug out I mean disciplining a child in such a way that he accepts responsibility and learns accountability for his actions.

So, how does all this Reality Discipline business work? Let me give you a recent example from my own family. We faced a situation where it was necessary to clean up the backyard in a very few minutes. Our home was for sale and a realtor was bringing a prospective buyer. The problem was the backyard looked as if it has been used for maneuvers by the Russian army. The dog had torn up paper plates and had also deposited several of what we like to euphemistically call "dog flops." I rounded up Holly and Kristin, my two older children, and asked them to help me get the yard cleaned up.

"Let's get all those paper plates raked up," I said. "And all the dog flops, too. Let's hurry. The real estate people will be here in a few minutes."

My request did not meet with the cries of joyful anticipation. Picking up dog flops is not a chore that our children relish. But if you have a dog, you face the reality of dog flops in your yard (or angry neighbors!). And if the family is going to enjoy the dog, the reality is that the family must take care of the dog—and his flops.

On this particular day, neither one of my daughters was interested in facing reality. They immediately got into a big hassle about who was going to do what, who had picked up dog flops last, etc., etc., ad bedlam.

In my mind's eye I could practically see the real estate agent and the prospective buyers of the house turning into the driveway. What was I, the skilled psychologist (with thirteen years of college!) to do? What I did was to stop my daughters in the middle of their argument and firmly escort them into the house, where I told them that I didn't want their help and that they could sit in the house and do whatever they wanted to do.

At this point you might be thinking, *This is Reality Discipline? It sounds pretty permissive to me—looks as if Leman gave up.*

Actually I was using one of the principles of Reality Discipline. Yes, I could have bawled them out, or even spanked them, but I don't believe any of these would have achieved the kind of guiding and training I was after. To be honest, I wanted to give them the opportunity to get in touch with their consciences concerning their behavior. I wanted to help them see the reality of the situation, which called for several people cooperating to get a job done in a short period of time.

"Okay, girls," I said. "If you don't want to help, you don't have to. I'll do the job alone."

Fortunately, the real estate agent and prospective buyers did not come wheeling up in the next few minutes. Within five minutes, one daughter came out to the backyard and started picking up dog flops without saying a word. In a few more minutes, the other daughter came out and asked, "Daddy, can I help you clean up the backyard, too? May I, please?"

Did you hear that question? Five minutes before, they both were hassling about picking up dog flops, and now one of them was picking them up and the other was begging me to *please* let her help.

After we cleaned up the yard and the real estate agent and prospective buyers had come and gone (they didn't buy the house, by the way), I talked with Holly and Kris about why I had become upset with their behavior.

"I love you girls very, very much," I said. "But there are certain situations when we've got to cooperate. When you start to fight and argue, I would rather not have you around, and that's why I told you to just go in the house. But I am proud of your coming out to volunteer to help."

Now you may be viewing this whole scene and saying, "Wonderful, Leman. You told your girls to go in the house and forget helping because they were being unpleasant. If I told my kids that, they'd be out the other door and down the street and I wouldn't see them for three hours. My kids just don't get in touch with their consciences that easily. Reality for me is that I would have cleaned up the whole yard myself."

Okay, I hear you and I can see your point. I only use this incident to demonstrate a principle from Reality Discipline that is based on the scriptural teaching that talks about heaping coals of fire upon the head (Proverbs 25:21, 22). When I confronted that "I don't wanna pick up dog flops" scene, I was working on a base of previous loving discipline and training. I wanted to confront my girls with the need to be more mature and responsible. And so, instead of screaming at them or giving them a swat and telling them to get to work, I marched them into the house and let them know that their attitude and behavior were disappointing. And they knew me well enough to know that they could come back out and offer to help when they were ready.

And that is what Reality Discipline—discipline with love—is all about. It's sometimes tough to pull off. Frankly, I gambled. They might have stayed in the house, and if they had, I would have cleaned up the yard myself and then talked to them later about the entire incident. They both knew the dog flops were a regular chore for which they were responsible. If they had refused to help at all, I probably would have paid myself out of their allowances for working on their behalf. Essentially, I had given them a choice: do the work yourself or pay for the privilege of having someone do the work for you. I really like that principle because it is so much like life.

I believe Reality Discipline is Ephesians 6:4 in action: not driving your kids up the wall as you make them ride on a yo-yo of inconsistency—permissive one minute and harsh the next. Reality Discipline takes patience, skill, and a commitment to wanting to train and guide, not simply blow your cool and vent your anger and call it "discipline."

I believe Reality Discipline keeps us right on line with our heavenly Father. God's love for us is *unconditional*. He loves us just because we are who we are—imperfect and prone to make mistakes. And He wants us to love our children in the same unconditional way. The desire to love as unconditionally as possible is prerequisite number one for a parent who wants to practice Reality Discipline.

Prerequisite number two is to be willing to take the time to practice it! As I deal with parents and their children, I see again and again the lack of commitment to take the time to discipline properly. We live in a society that gives us instant everything, and we seem to think we can have "instant good behavior" from our kids as well. But it takes time to raise a child to be a responsible citizen.

As veteran youth speaker Mel Johnson puts it, "Parenthood is a long-term investment, not a short-term loan." Parenthood is knowing the joy of success, the sting of failure, and the frustration of the "near miss." They all come with the territory, especially when you practice Reality Discipline. But I believe Reality Discipline is the best way to guide—not drive—your little ones to real maturity, where they can function as responsible adults.

As I just said, you will have successes, failures, and near misses, but that's what this book is all about. It gives you freedom—freedom to make mistakes, freedom to "blow it" now and then. And I hope it teaches you to give your children that same kind of freedom. I'm not talking about being permissive. As you will see, I am the archenemy of permissiveness. In chapter 1 we are going to take a look at the rotten fruit of permissiveness and its antidote: real love and discipline.

In the first half of this book we will be looking at the principles and strategy behind Reality Discipline. We'll explore such topics as:

How to be the authority in your home without being authoritarian.

How children learn.

Why reward and punishment no longer work.

The second part of the book will deal with specific ways to use Reality Discipline in the everyday hassles that come with parenting. We will cover everything from fighting to forgetting, from talking back to taming the TV monster.

But one word of caution. Please don't skip the first several chapters so you can get right into the "practical stuff" and get instant answers. Learn the principles that underlie the whole Reality Discipline concept. I have put plenty of practical illustrations into these first chapters as well. You're probably going to find some humorous parts, and some spots where you say, "Oh, that's me! That's us—that's our neighbors or our friends."

And oh, yes, one more important point. As you read this book, feel free to reject my suggestions or modify them. If something I say doesn't quite make sense for you in your family or your situation, put it aside. Put it on the shelf for a while. Use the parts and the ideas that do make sense. You know your children best. You be the judge of what works for them as you try to love them unconditionally.

I'm totally convinced that many of us so-called experts have done too much to confuse parents rather than give them freedom and real help. I don't want to be a part of that. I want to offer things that will be of practical benefit to you as you deal on a day-to-day basis with those special gifts from God—your children.

Part One

Why Reality Discipline Will Work in Your Home

1

Inconsistency—or How to Raise a Yo-Yo

Do you remember that fantastic day when your first child came into the world? I'll never forget the experience of watching my daughter's birth. What a joy it was to realize I was part of creating that miracle gift of God. My wife, Sande, joined me in celebration. All the apprehension and pain of the hours of labor evaporated when little Holly was placed in her arms—twenty and one-half inches long and as cute as they come. In the next few days, I proudly showed Holly to all my friends, and I had no trouble at all coming to the conclusion that she was the most beautiful baby in the entire nursery.

We took Holly home on the third day, and for the occasion, friends put a huge sign across the front of the house that read, WELCOME HOME, HOLLY! To say I was an excited new father would be understating it quite a bit. My wife still teases me about the first night, when we placed Holly in her bassinet beside our bed. I turned up the thermostat so high it was 105 degrees in the house!

Okay, okay, so I turned the heat up a little too high. Better to be on the safe side, was my motto. I was a new parent and I knew my responsibility: to take care of this totally dependent little girl.

No wonder I was puzzled when that very same week Sande's obstetrician advised us, "I want both of you to start leaving your daughter home with a baby-sitter sometime during the first few weeks of her life." I had to ask him to repeat the comment. Besides being a difficult assignment, it seemed totally inappropriate. At the very height of our newborn's dependency, our doctor was suggesting we leave her and go out for the evening.

But since then I've thanked God many times for that word of advice from the doctor. In the wisdom accumulated over many years, he knew that if Sande and I were to truly love Holly we would need to be sure to maintain a strong love between ourselves. He knew that the stronger we were as man and wife the stronger we would be as parents. So, in those very first weeks we started to develop the one essential ingredient for effective discipline in our home: love. And those first few weeks were a perfect time to begin to discipline ourselves and our new child.

And the discipline wasn't easy. It is no small trick to leave your newborn at home. Finding a baby-sitter was a major problem. There seems to be a tendency on the part of young couples to think that the only baby-sitter qualified to care for their child is a registered nurse who specializes in pediatrics or, of course, Grandma! But Sande and I took her doctor's advice and disciplined ourselves to go out at least one night a week and leave Holly home with a sitter.

I hate to think what might have happened if we had ignored our doctor's advice and centered our every move around our firstborn child. I'm quite sure Holly wouldn't be the responsible child she is today at age eleven. She would have been like many of the children I see weekly in my private practice. These children have been brought up with the philosophy that says, "Love, love, love . . . if I just *love* little Buford enough, everything will be all right." But everything isn't all right. Children who have been given love without discipline are often disrespectful and/or too dependent on their parents.

What Christian Nurture Is Not

Many parents—particularly from Christian homes—often get brainwashed with the idea that Christian nurture is built on doing everything for their children and making all decisions for them. Mothers or fathers caught in this trap might be overheard saying, "I don't care if you *are* fifteen years old, stand still! I'm going to button your shirt." If you want disaster and chaos in your life, do *everything* for your children. In the process, you will rob them of the opportunity to stand on their own two feet and to learn responsibility and accountability, two qualities that are vital in developing a well-balanced adult life.

But let's get back to our infant Holly for a moment. Was Sande's doctor telling us that we should neglect Holly, or fail to give her a lot of tender care, cuddling, holding, and so on? Of course not. All of that is absolutely critical. We psychologists call the tender loving care given by parents—particularly the mother—in the first weeks and months of life, a time of bonding. It's during this time that the parent conveys to the totally dependent infant the fact that he or she is cared for and loved. Many studies have shown that permanent damage can be done to the personality of a newborn baby if tactual stimulating, loving, and cuddling aren't present in the first few critical days and months of life.

But what Sande's doctor was telling us was that even during infancy a parent needs to start building discipline into a child's life. By going out one night a week and leaving Holly with a baby-sitter, we began a routine that Holly soon could detect, even at her tender age. Putting a child on a schedule of one kind or another—for example, feeding, sleeping—begins to put order into the child's life. The schedule can be flexible but it still can teach the child order. And as the child learns order, he also learns responsibility and accountability—he learns where he fits into the entire scheme of things and what his responsibilities are.

As I give seminars on family living, parenthood, and discipline throughout the United States and Canada, I'm frequently asked questions that can be summed up in these words: "Why can't we, the parents, just make all the decisions for our kids? We know what's best for them."

I sympathize with parents who ask those questions, because I'm a parent myself. Parents do feel that they truly do know what's best for their children. And as we seek to convey love and concern to our children, we want to guide them away from some of the pitfalls of life and getting hurt. But at the same time, we should want to teach our children that they can make some mistakes. Children need to know they have the right to fail. They need opportunities to make decisions about their own lives.

Authoritarians Make All the Decisions

Many parents don't like this "freedom to fail" concept when I present it in a seminar. A few years ago, as I was speaking on the topic "Establishing the authority of God and the parent in the home," a man jumped up and interrupted, "Hey, Leman! You've gone far enough! I've heard enough of this garbage. I know what's best for my children and I'll make all decisions for them, thank you. I don't go for this giving a kid an opportunity to make decisions that can really affect his life."

I understood how that father felt, but I also knew he needed to think about what he was really saying. And so I asked him, "Who is going to make the decision for your child to accept Jesus Christ as Lord and Savior?" The father sat down. He knew he couldn't make that decision for anyone but himself.

What I wanted that father to see is that there are some decisions we can only make for ourselves. In fact, as we grow up and get older, there should be more and more decisions that we make for ourselves. I believe that a critical need in homes today is that they become the kind of environment in which children can learn more about themselves. Home should be a place where children can make mistakes as they try out some things they have decided *on their own.*

Remember Ephesians 6:1–4, the passage I quoted back in the foreword? I said it would be the base for everything we would talk about. I particularly enjoy reading the first three verses. They're the kind I like to clip out, put on the refrigerator door, or pin to a child's pillowcase:

> Children, obey your parents; this is the right thing to do because God has placed them in authority over you. Honor your father and mother. This is the first of God's Ten Commandments that ends with a promise. And this is the promise: that if you honor your father and mother, yours will be a long life, full of blessing.
>
> Ephesians 6:1–3, TLB

But let's not forget the fourth verse of that passage. It has a lot to say about how we use our authority over our children, how we make decisions for them or allow them to make some themselves, and how we teach them responsibility in the home:

> And now a word to you parents. Don't keep on scolding and nagging your children, making them angry and resentful. Rather, bring them up with the loving discipline the Lord himself approves, with suggestions and godly advice.
>
> Ephesians 6:4, TLB

Authoritarianism Seems to Work

The Scripture tells us to be in authority over our children, but notice that it doesn't say to be *authoritarian.* Many of us grew up in authoritarian homes, or at least had parents who had been reared that way. Children don't have a lot of input into authoritarian systems. They just do as they're told and keep quiet. The confusing thing about authoritarianism is that it often *seems* to work. The typical pattern in an author-

itarian home is a pecking order that seems to indicate that
men are better than women and adults are better than
children.

There was a time—between thirty and fifty years ago—
when our society supported the authoritarian concept. But
as a certain advertisement tells us, "We've come a long way,
baby." The problem in 1984 America is that children no
longer view themselves as "inferior" to adults. They have
learned to speak up and speak out and they often feel they
are the equal of any adult. There is a sense, of course, in
which we are all equal to one another—particularly in
God's eyes. But when children feel they are the same as
adults with regard to living in a household and playing a
particular role in that household, the word *authority* begins
to take on strange shapes and twisted meanings.

As I counsel families, I see evidence every week of how
today's children are not really programmed to respond well
to authoritarianism or permissiveness. In both cases, their
feelings of "being equal" to Mom and Dad get in the way.
Over and over, I see disciplinary problems in the homes
where authoritarianism is practiced on a daily basis or
where, at the other end of the continuum, the children are
allowed to run free by totally permissive parents.

When we deal with children from an authoritarian view-
point, we come at them with the general attitude that we
know what's best for them, we can make all their decisions
for them, and they essentially don't have the wherewithal to
make the kinds of decisions that life requires. The authoritarian parent often backs up his "I know best" attitude with
force, but that's not what the "loving discipline" of Ephesians 6:4 is talking about. Perhaps the most misused (not to
mention misquoted) verse in the Bible is, "Spare the rod and
spoil the child." The actual text reads: "He who spares the
rod hates his son, but he who loves him is careful to discipline him" (Proverbs 13:24, NIV).

The Jews believed in discipline, true, but when biblical
writers used the word *rod* they were thinking more of cor-

rection and guidance rather than hitting and beating. For example, the shepherd used his rod not to beat his sheep but to guide them. We are all well acquainted with that phrase from the Twenty-third Psalm, "thy rod and thy staff they comfort me" (verse 4, KJV). But I doubt that many of us would feel very comforted if the Lord's rod was waling away at our heads or bottoms at every wrong turn we made.

Another thing that concerns me about the "spare the rod" philosophy is that it is based on *controlling* children rather than truly nurturing them. I've seen far too many examples of well-meaning parents—often from Christian homes— who dominate their children verbally and physically. There is some strange confusion in the minds of many parents about what makes a child "good" or well behaved. They seem to prefer the child who is submissive, palatable, and easy to lead—sort of like a puppy.

I, too, want my children to be well behaved, but I'm not so sure I want them to be easily controlled by others. My children will soon be moving into adolescence, and I want them to be ready. I want them to be ready for that turbulent world where they will be buffeted by the changing winds of peer-group pressure. I want them to be able to stand, to be responsible and mature, and to think for themselves. But if all I have done while they are young is to control and domi-nate them, they will be at a serious disadvantage. I prefer the concepts of Reality Discipline, which give my children many opportunities to make decisions, and there is no better place to learn how to make decisions than at home. I believe home should be a place where children can learn to fail and then pick themselves up and go forward. Above all, I want them to be able to make the supreme decision for life: to ac-cept Jesus Christ as Savior and then trust Him as Lord on a day-to-day basis.

Let me repeat that while I am critical of authoritarianism and its overuse of the "rod," I am not saying that I don't be-lieve in taking the necessary action to discipline the child in a loving way. Sometimes—and we must be careful to know just when it really fits—spanking is the necessary action. I'll talk more about this in chapter 4. But the important thing is that the parent move quickly in every case to give the child the guidance and direction he needs to become a responsible and accountable person. If the parent fails to go into action, he winds up at the other end of the spectrum: permissiveness.

Permissiveness Reaps Rebellion

The permissive parent essentially says, "Oh, do your own thing. Whatever you want is okay." My years of counseling parents and children have shown me that in a permissive environment the kids rebel. They rebel because they feel anger and hatred toward their parents for a lack of guidelines and limit setting. Many parents might challenge me here, but I believe the children want order in their lives and even if given the opportunity to "do anything they want" they eventually come back to dead center.

In one study involving elementary grades, the children were allowed to eat anything they wanted in the cafeteria over a period of thirty days. The study showed that although the children predictably would "pig out" on sweets and other junk food at first, after a few weeks, they tended to go back to a quite balanced diet. I believe this study indicates the need children have for order and balance in their lives. I'm not saying that you can always give children unlimited freedom to do whatever they want, but I am saying that in certain conditions when a child does have the freedom to make choices, he learns how to make those choices in a sensible and accountable way.

One afternoon, I sat in my office listening to the parents of Ronny, age eleven, who told me they were forced to lock up all their valuables (including their wallets!) in a safe-deposit box at the bank. The reason for this was simple:

Ronny was stealing his parents blind. It seemed he had a heavy video-game-machine habit and also liked to indulge himself in various treats.

Ronny's behavior might have been understandable if his parents had never given him any money to manage by himself, but that wasn't the case. Ronny had always had an allowance.

Perhaps his parents were unkind to him? No, that wasn't the problem either.

One day while I had both parents in a therapy session, the mother gave me the clue I needed. She told me rather proudly, "You know, we've never left Ronny home alone."

My response was, "That's unfortunate."

At first, the mother didn't understand what I was saying, but as we talked, she got the point. By giving constant attention, his parents had robbed him of the opportunity to stand on his own two feet and be responsible. And so, at eleven years old he was behaving in a totally irresponsible manner and in a way that was very hurtful toward his parents.

In classic permissive style, Ronny's folks couldn't understand what was going on. They told me, "We've given Ronny everything he's ever asked for; we've tried to provide everything for him."

What a tragic misunderstanding of true parental love! Love isn't giving your kid everything he wants. If there's one thing I'm becoming convinced of, it's this: today in our society we are raising too many children to be "takers." They don't know the meaning of the word *give,* but they use another word over and over: *gimme, gimme, gimme!*

There Is a Middle Ground

We've talked quite a bit about the extremes of authoritarian and permissive parenting. We know instinctively, and through countless examples, that neither extreme works very well. What a lot of parents seem to do, however, is wander inconsistently between the two—permissive to a point, then cracking down with authoritarian wrath. I see a lot of parents in this bind. They dangle their child on a yo-yo of inconsistency, and then wonder why the kid often acts like a "yo-yo."

So, what can parents do? How do they stop the inconsistent swing between authoritarianism and permissiveness? How do they find a middle ground that makes sense to them—and to their child? There are a number of names for that middle ground, but the one I like best is *authoritative.* Don't confuse *authoritative* with *authoritarian.* There is a world of difference. Authoritative parents do not dominate their children and make all decisions for them. Instead, they use the principles of Reality Discipline, which are tailor-made to give children the loving correction and training the Lord approves (Ephesians 6:4).

How does it all work? Well, suppose your seven-year-old breaks a toy belonging to another child. What should you do? What type of discipline is needed in this situation? I believe the discipline ought to be based on *reality.* The reality of this situation is that if you break someone else's property, you pay for it.

Now, you may be thinking, *Dr. Leman must be kidding. A seven-year-old kid, pay for a toy?* I'm not kidding at all. Your seven-year-old can come up with the money. It comes out of his allowance or his bank account. You'd be amazed at how many children have bank accounts before age seven. Grandmas and grandpas make a science of keeping just this kind of account afloat.

So, if your seven-year-old breaks another child's toy, you can lovingly discipline him by holding him accountable. He learns that this type of behavior costs him money.

Of course, you could give him a swat or even a good, hard spanking. You could scream at him, demean him, call him names, and send him to his room. All of these would be what I call punishment. Punishment centers in on the child and misses the real problem. When we punish a child, we indicate to him that we don't like him or love him. But with Reality Discipline, you can hold the child accountable for what he has chosen to do as you teach him the consequences of making a poor decision.

And so, in our own home, when one of our children breaks a toy, it doesn't matter whether it belongs to him or to someone else. We do not run out and buy another one to replace it. That would simply teach him or her to be irresponsible. Our children would soon get the idea they could break anything they wanted and tear up anything they wanted to and there would always be someone there to replace it for them. I say that is not realistic. Good discipline is always based upon the reality of the situation. And in this situation, reality says, "You broke the toy; now you pay for another one out of your allowance."

In chapter 3, I will be expanding on how to use the allowance as a teaching and disciplinary tool, and it's amazing how all this works. In so many situations, you can let reality be the teacher if you only stand back and allow reality to happen.

I believe that parenting and disciplining children in an authoritative way involves at least three things:

1. *Discipline by way of action.* The discipline should be swift, direct, effective, and as closely tied to the violation of the family rule as possible. An example is what we have just talked about. When a toy is broken, it should be replaced, paid for, or mended.

2. *Parents must listen to their children.* There is great power in listening, but few of us tap that source of power. It's just too easy not to listen—to our children, to our spouses, to just about anyone. Or, when we do try to hear what they say, we're really not listening at a feeling level and that means we're really not listening at all. I got a dramatic lesson in what it means to not be listening in a conversation I had with my own daughter. At the time I was the guest psychologist on "The Toni Tennille Show," which was then broad-

cast on national television. I invited Holly, our oldest daughter, to come with me to see the show.

Holly said, "Daddy, I would really like to come to the show."

I said, "Well, honey, that's why I invited you. I thought it would be a good idea to have you see how they put together a TV show, what a real television studio is like, and all that."

There were several seconds of dead silence and when I looked at Holly I saw tears in her eyes. I said, "Holly! What's wrong?"

Holly said, "Daddy, that's not what I mean."

"Well, what do you mean?" I replied.

She responded, "Daddy, after you go on TV with Toni Tennille, maybe could I just sing one song?"

Whoa! It was obvious I hadn't been listening. Holly was saying she wanted to go to the show, all right. She wanted to *be on* the show. She wanted to sing on national television! I hadn't been tuned to her wavelength at all. And once tuned in, I then faced the formidable task of helping Holly understand "reality." Gently but firmly I had to explain that I didn't have the authority to let her sing on the show, but I certainly hoped she would come along with me to watch. She finally understood!

This little incident could be passed over as just a "lack of communication." But I prefer to see it as a beautiful example of how real listening takes training. We've got to be aware of our children and how they perceive life. (We'll be looking more at this in the next chapter.)

3. *Parents should give themselves to their children.* Giving of yourself (not things) to your children is an essential ingredient for effective discipline. Many times parents apologetically ask me, "What do I have to offer my children?" I always respond, "You have yourself."

The simple truth is, children want us. They want our time. But time is very precious and most of us seem to run out of it too soon. Isn't it ironic that we often run out of enough time for our children? We somehow think that we can get together with them later. Perhaps we can start to spend more time in a few months, or possibly after the first of the year when the job settles down. Strangely enough the time never seems to magically appear. As we rush through life, time gets even more precious. And before we know it, our children are into teenage years and then grown and gone, and we never did get to know them. Instead, we tried to discipline them without really knowing who they were.

I frequently hear parents talking about "quality time." I understand what parents mean by that, but in all my years of private practice I've never heard one of my young clients (the children) mention "quality time." All a child knows is that he wants your time and your attention, whether it's to watch him do somersaults and cartwheels or to take him for a Big Mac. In trying to find time for your children, don't worry too much about how much "quality" is in it. Give them all the time you can and the quality will take care of itself. And as you give them time, you will get to know them. You will be able to build a base for action-oriented and loving discipline.

In summary, never forget that children expect adults to discipline them. If the discipline is loving, it will be geared toward instruction, teaching, guiding, and, above all, holding a child accountable for his or her actions.

When a parent doesn't discipline a child, that parent invites rebellion. In essence, he is giving the child a license to hold his parents in contempt. Children can actually develop hatred toward their parents if the parents don't take a stand and discipline them.

But if we take that stand, the payoff is tremendous. The following note sums it all up. It was written by that little girl you met when this chapter opened. She is that same little girl whom we started to "discipline" in the very first weeks of her life by taking one night a week to get a baby-sitter in order to keep our marriage in good repair.

When Holly was seven years old, she gave me the following note for Father's Day. The original hangs on my office wall:

> World's gatist father,
>
> My father is the gratist,
> for your the best,
> caring, Loveing,
> THE BEST! ! ! ! !
> even when you disaplin' me,
> I Love you the same,
>
> Love,
> HOLLY

Holly's spelling needs a little work, but—for her dad—the content more than makes up for it. Naturally, I like the "World's gatist father" line, but I am more impressed by something else. It's interesting to me that Holly used the term *discipline* rather than the word *punish*. Children *want* us to discipline them because the act of discipline shows them we care.

2

It's All in the Eye of the Beholder

When thinking about Reality Discipline, it's always good to stop and grapple with a basic question: What is reality?

As a high school student, I was once called on to give testimony in court concerning an auto accident I had witnessed. As a seventeen-year-old, I remember thinking how odd it was that two other witnesses to the accident could be so blind. I *knew* I was right. The car at fault was the blue one, not the red one they had identified. And the blue car was headed east, not west!

Way back in high school, in that courtroom, I learned firsthand about the concept that is often called "the eye of the beholder." Parenting your child with Reality Discipline has its "eye of the beholder" element also. One of your major goals in using Reality Discipline is to help your child think and learn. But in order to be successful, you have to understand what reality is—particularly for your child. No matter what you, the adult, think or know about a given situation, as far as discipline is concerned, reality is how your child views that situation. What precisely happened, or what precisely is going on, is not really the issue. It is what a child *thinks* that counts. Your child's perception of what is happening is the reality you must deal with.

32

In this chapter, I want to talk about three seemingly unrelated areas. All three, however, give crucial insights on how children learn and what reality is—as they see it. (For more information on birth order and its effects on personality development and marriage happiness, see my books *Parenthood Without Hassles—Well, Almost,* published by Harvest House, and *Sex Begins in the Kitchen,* published by Regal Books.)

They Learn Through Birth Order

In chapter 1 we took a look at how children perceive us when we dangle them on a yo-yo of inconsistency, somewhere between being authoritarian and permissive. The happy middle ground is the authoritative approach, which I believe is epitomized in the principles of Reality Discipline. When you use Reality Discipline, you have to be much more aware of your child's perceptions and you have to learn how to understand and relate to each child and his or her special needs.

That's why I think it's so critical to understand that the order of birth has tremendous implications for how each child in your family learns and perceives reality. It is safe to say that each child perceives his or her family differently, because each child operates from a different vantage point within the family. For example, the firstborn child has only adult models to learn from: Mom and Dad. These adult models often do things so well that it's no surprise firstborn children tend to be much like "little adults."

A great deal of psychological research has been done on personality traits of children in different birth positions within the family. Firstborns are often achievers. They tend to walk and talk earlier and they have a larger vocabulary at a younger age. It's no surprise that later on—in high school, college, and adult life—honor societies are often glutted with firstborn children.

Firstborns tend to be perfectionistic and will face new situations and challenges with a great deal of caution. First-borns don't like making mistakes. Perhaps you can recall those times in your own life when you were in the classroom and knew the answer to the question, but for one reason or another, you didn't want to speak up. This is a very common trait among firstborn children. Firstborns have a unique need to be right and "perfect" every time.

Second-born children tend to be the opposite of firstborns in many ways. The second-born usually has life a little bit easier than his older brother or sister, who has probably served as something of a guinea pig. Mom and Dad essentially experiment with the firstborn child. The firstborn is brought up with stricter rules and regulations. The expectations are higher for firstborns than for those who come later. That's why firstborns often seem more reliable and conscientious than the siblings who come after them.

Second-borns often wind up as the "middle child." Because they seem to wind up "in the middle" in just about everything, they tend to be mediators. Middle-born children like to avoid conflict as much as they can, but they are not weaklings by any sense of the term. They usually know how to fend for themselves because they have landed between two very special people in the family—the oldest and the youngest. Parents may not like to admit it but they tend to give the middle-born child less attention and therefore he learns to be more independent in all kinds of circumstances.

The child born third in the family often winds up the youngest. This youngest child tends to be outgoing, personable, and manipulative. Because he is the "baby" of the family, he is skilled at manipulating others. Just ask any firstborn child. He will tell you that the baby of the family is the one who gets away with murder!

Granted, all of my observations on the tendencies of first, second, and third-born children are just that—descriptions of their "tendencies." There are no guarantees that children will act or develop in a certain way, no matter where they are born in the family sequence. Nonetheless, many studies bear out the validity of these general descriptions. What is important is that parents realize that each of their children has a different perception of life and reality, and much of this perception depends on where they land in the birth order. It's important, also, to see that with every birth or addition to the family, the entire family changes. With the birth of each child, the family unit becomes an entirely new and different entity.

The key questions for parents to keep asking as each child comes along are: "Are we making each of our children feel loved and appreciated? Are we aware of the pressures and tensions working on our family?"

There is, for example, the problem of the "dethronement" of the firstborn when the second child comes along. In my counseling practice with families, I see a continual syndrome: the firstborn child is usually overparented. He gets too much attention. Thousands of photographs (it seems) are taken. He is definitely kingpin. Then along comes his little brother or sister and all of a sudden he seems left out in the cold. He isn't allowed to touch baby brother or sister. He can't help feed or cuddle the new arrival. And now Mommy doesn't seem to have much time for him at all because she is too busy with this new little "intruder."

Two key ways of helping your firstborn child feel less intruded upon are through communication and involvement. Mom should talk to her firstborn while she is pregnant and explain what is happening and just what is growing inside her tummy. She can let the firstborn feel his little brother or sister kicking inside.

In every way she can, many months before the second child arrives, Mother can be programming her firstborn to be prepared for baby brother or sister and to be aware that the new arrival is going to take some of Mom's time, too.

Once the second-born child arrives, the parents should do everything they can to involve the firstborn in its care. Even if the firstborn is barely two years old, Mother should let him touch and caress and help in any way possible. Just allowing the firstborn child to "help hold the bottle" while feeding the new baby can be very significant.

And, when Mom gets busy with the new baby, she should continually reassure the firstborn that he is important, too. And don't forget ways Dad can help by doing something special with the firstborn to make him feel extra important and loved.

As each child comes along, he or she will seek ways to identify his place in the family and ultimately in society. If each child feels loved, appreciated, and cared for, he will feel good about himself. As he goes off to preschool or kindergarten, he is much better equipped for the battle.

Parents should realize that each child's personality will chiefly be influenced by the sibling who is least like him. Take, for example, a male child who has a bright and articulate brother who is one and a half years older. Suppose older brother does very well in school (something that is not uncommon for firstborn children). The second-born child may be discouraged by his brother's abilities and not do as well with his schoolwork. He may have equal ability but feel intimidated and threatened by older brother's accomplishments. So, he withdraws from the academic arena, which isn't as safe or as enjoyable. The second-born usually tries to find recognition in other ways. If his older brother is the scholar, he may decide to be the athlete. There are dozens of possible ways children can go. What is typical is that the second-born often chooses to specialize in a field where he won't have to go head-to-head in competition with an older brother or sister.

One thing is certain: each child is unique. God creates each one with special qualities and his or her own personality. My own daughters, Holly and Kris, are eighteen months apart. It has always been fascinating to watch them go into a store to pick out a toy or a treat. If we let her, Holly would stand there for an hour and a half and look at every possibility. She would read the directions, compare weights and sizes, and so on and on. Krissy, on the other hand, usually picks out what she wants in a few minutes or less. This is just one simple illustration about how a firstborn (Holly) is careful and calculating, while the second-born (Krissy) tends to be more of a "free spirit."

Observe your own children and note their differences. More important, be aware of how you are responding to those differences. Are you tending to favor one child over another, in even the most subtle ways? Children are amazingly perceptive. And remember what I said as this chapter opened: reality for your child is what he or she perceives—no more and no less. It is absolutely critical that we communicate to each one of our children, despite any differences among them, that we love and care for them *just because they are who they are.* If Reality Discipline is to work in your home, the ideal at which you must always aim is unconditional love for each child. That's why it's always absolutely vital to discipline a child by making him accountable for his actions instead of punishing the child with verbal or physical abuse.

They Learn by Taking "Power Trips"

Every young mother knows how frustrating it can be to spend all day at home with one or more young children. It usually gets to you in one way or another. For example, it's not uncommon to hear two young mothers chatting over a cup of coffee and have one say, "Excuse me, Mary Jane, but I have to go potty." More than one young mother has confessed to me that she is ready to crack up for want of some adult conversation.

That's why I think it's crucial for young parents to find time for themselves apart from their children during the week. (Remember our doctor's advice to get a baby-sitter for Holly when she was just a few weeks old?) One of the best programs ever devised is one that I've seen started in many churches. It is usually called something like, "Mother's Morning Out." Young mothers have the opportunity to bring their children to church and have them cared for while Mom goes wherever she would like for the morning. I can think of no more practical way for a church to serve a community than to allow young mothers the opportunity to get apart from their children for a few hours.

I also believe that fathers can think of no more practical way to show love for their wives than to help with the children whenever possible. Dad can come home from work early and allow Mom to get away to do something by herself. He can take the kids to the pediatrician and on any other number of errands. He can say, now and then, "Honey, sit down for dinner and I'll do all the serving." *That,* gentlemen, is how to really make love to your wife! As I often tell the fathers I counsel, "A man's place *is* in the home."

Getting away for even a few hours may sound great to many mothers, but some of them might wonder, *What if my child needs me?* That's just the point. Your child does not need you *all of the time.* Parents and children need minivacations from one another on a regular basis. I always tell young mothers to get all the rest they can. (They usually laugh hysterically, but I mean what I say.) Mother needs to treat herself fairly and not become a slave to her children. If Mom is always there to meet every little need the child has, the child soon becomes psychologically crippled by believing that he can exist only with Mom's presence. Another part of the "Mom is always there" syndrome is that the child learns there is a payoff in crying and fussing. The child learns that he can be very powerful, that he can use tears to manipulate Mommy and even Daddy by overly involving them in his life.

As I counsel parents and their children, I see repeated illustrations of how children learn through experimenting with power. Psychiatrist Alfred Adler calls it "purposive behavior." Adler observes that *all* social behavior has a purpose. With children, the purpose is often a maladaptive one: to keep Mom and Dad at bay, or to keep them needlessly involved in his life. To put it in today's jargon, the child takes "power trips" to see who is going to dominate, control, win, or "be the boss." And with every power trip, the child learns a little more about what works and doesn't work with Mom and Dad.

Adler points out that the very shy child can still be a very powerful child. The child uses his shyness to invoke Mom and Dad's sympathy and to get them involved in his life. And by "involved" I mean overinvolved. All children are self-centered and they tend to be concerned about number one at all times. At very young ages in particular, they can't get enough of Mom or Dad and they will do everything they can to keep them dangling on a string of concern and anxiety. Show me a shy kid and I'll usually show you a very powerful little character.

Other children may use tears or temper tantrums to make their parents respond to them in certain ways. Children can actually become miniature bullies as they needlessly involve adults in their lives.

Another way to describe a child's "power trips" is to simply realize that children are always going to seek attention. They want our attention; they need adult attention; and they are going to get that attention one way or another. Ask any schoolteacher: "Do children seek attention?" He or she will always answer, "Of course they do!" And they get that attention by positive or negative means. If a child doesn't find his place at school with positive means such as making good grades, he may call attention to himself in negative ways which cause teachers to send home notes to Mom and to make "needs improvement" notations on report cards.

Another weapon some children use to gain attention is the "I'm so discouraged" approach. Some children become quite adept at playing on Mom's sympathy as they take little power trips in the form of pity parties.

All of these behaviors are what psychologists refer to as "powerful." Powerful behavior is a child's way of saying to the parent and other adults, "I can control you. I can dominate you. I can win. I can make you do anything I want."

Powerful behavior is particularly distressing to parents. Most parents are well aware of when a child is "doing a number" on them. Feelings well up inside of us that say, "You *can't* do that to me! Don't you know who *I* am? I'm your father"—or "I'm your mother!"

Many problems between parents and their children begin right here, as the children start to experiment with power. When a child gets to that stage (anywhere from two years of age on up), he realizes he has power and he tests—with *all* his might—the limits being imposed upon him within the family. One classic form of testing is the temper tantrum. If parents can deal with these initial power plays appropriately, they will prevent a lot of problems further down the line. When a child uses his temper to say, "I'm going to control you, Mom and Dad," they had better be ready to deal with the child swiftly, *and with action, not just words.*

Suppose, for example, your child has a temper tantrum while you're busy trying to prepare dinner. How do you handle it with action and not just words? Obviously you don't do a lot of pleading and imploring for the child to stop. And you certainly don't want to bribe the child with a cookie or some other reward. All of this simply reinforces his attempt to gain power and control over you.

What about spanking? Is this effective? Usually the answer is no. Spanking only increases the octaves and volume of the temper tantrum. And the child only learns that he can still control his mom or dad to some degree, even if it gains him a negative reward. In chapter 4, I'll be saying more about spanking as a legitimate disciplinary tool. Right here, however, I want to underline the fact that spanking does little good when a temper tantrum is in progress.

I believe the best approach to a temper tantrum is for the parent to pick up the child and place him in his room. Close the door behind him and let him know that he is free to have his temper tantrum in private, and that when he has calmed down, he can rejoin you or the rest of the family. It may even be necessary to remove the child from the home. Let him know that he can have his temper tantrum in the backyard and when he is finished he may come back into the house.

What do these "isolation methods" accomplish? What they say to the child is, "All right, you are having a temper tantrum, and I'm not going to stop you. But you are not going to control me by making me listen. When you can be more agreeable, we can get back together."

When you attempt to try and stop a temper tantrum with pleading, arguing, scolding, or spanking, you usually wind up with the child becoming more powerful and out of control. (Actually he is *in* control, but he seems out of control to you.) But, if you have the courage to pick up your child and place him outside the room or the house, you can be almost positive the temper tantrum will vanish immediately. Why? Because you've taken the source of power away: you have separated yourself from the scene the child is making for your benefit.

Here is the epitome of Reality Discipline. You are holding the child accountable for his decision to act inappropriately. You give him the right to act inappropriately, but *not in a social situation.* You have essentially told the child, "You can behave this way if you so choose, but you are going to do it alone and you are not going to disrupt my life and the lives of others around you."

This approach seldom fails. Children are not interested in using powerful behavior without an audience. The whole point in taking a power trip is to be sure to take Mom or Dad with you. If no one is along for the ride, the power trip is just no fun at all.

"Okay," you may be saying. "That may be a good idea for coping with a temper tantrum at home in my kitchen, but what do I do when we're out shopping?"

I appreciate the problem—I really do. I've had a few like that myself. What do you do when you are in the middle of a department store, or a supermarket checkout line, and your child suddenly goes bananas? There's little three-year-old Festus, kicking, screaming, biting, and slamming his fists on the floor. What do you do? If you reach down in anger and swat Festus, the temper tantrum simply heats up. The voice goes a few octaves higher and more people begin to gather to watch you and your child in the classic power struggle.

I tell mothers and fathers who face these public temper tantrums to do something very courageous: simply step *over* the child. (Granted, there is a great temptation to step *on* the child, but you are after positive results, not revenge.) Step over the child and walk toward the door. This sounds easy, but it could be the longest walk of your life. Take those first few steps, however, and I predict that your little one will be following you and asking you to wait. Why? Because a temper tantrum is not worth having if you don't have an audience to watch your performance.

Of course, there may be an audience of other shoppers who have started to crane their necks to watch you and Festus have at it. Hang in there and do not be manipulated. You can be sure that your child's real audience is you, not the other shoppers. He may try to embarrass you in front of the other people, but if you aren't buying, he will stop selling almost immediately. Just step over your child and walk away muttering something like, "Some people's children. . . ."

And what happens if your child *does not follow you?* Walk slowly, always keeping your eye on the child. If necessary, stop near the door and do a little browsing or go over next week's shopping list. Never let him or her out of your sight, but put a good amount of distance between you so he no longer has the audience he wants: you. Eventually (before the week is out?) he will discover he's "lost"!

If the child's temper-tantrum behavior continues on other trips to the store, you may have to resort to leaving him at home. Arrange for a baby-sitter and explain to the child exactly why he is being left at home. Simply say, "Mommy's leaving you home because of how disruptive you get when we go to the store. When she has to take time out for your temper tantrums, she can't get her shopping done. When you can keep your temper better, you can go with Mommy again."

However you deal with powerful and purposive behavior, always keep in mind that every time your child takes a power trip, he or she is on another expedition of learning. He is learning about reality. If he gets away with his power plays, he learns that reality is manipulating and controlling Mom and Dad as much as possible. But if his power plays bear no fruit, he learns a different kind of reality. He learns that reality is being accountable for his actions and that unacceptable behavior has no payoff.

They Learn by Watching You

Perhaps the key way children learn as they perceive reality through their own eyes is by watching the adult role models around them. Obviously, their first role models are Mom and Dad. As they grow older, other significant adults become models: grandparents, brothers and sisters, aunts and uncles, teachers, playmates, the widow next door, and many others.

Some parents may argue with me, but I still believe that Mother and Dad always remain the key role models for their children. I realize the power of the peer group is great. And I realize that as children get older they often are deeply impressed by a certain teacher, coach, or even a movie star or professional athlete. But the ones they live with day in and day out are their parents. Your children do learn by watching you and, believe me, they watch much more carefully than you would ever imagine.

How then are parents to act as they go about the business of being "role models" day by day for their children? We all know the obvious answers: be a good example; be consistent; your actions speak louder than your words, and so on. I believe, however, that possibly the best way to be a good role model for your children is to be honest.

Children, you see, start out by being totally honest. They may learn deception and deviousness down the line, but they start out with a very open and honest approach to life.

I recall the time I discovered a local newspaper was dropping my family advice column in favor of one on dieting written by Richard Simmons. When my daughter Holly heard the news, she said, "Oh, good! I *like* Richard Simmons!" Yes, children can be totally honest, even when Dad's ego is on the line.

Sometimes a child's honesty can embarrass everyone concerned. When my son, Kevin, was nearly four years old, he stopped one day on the way home from preschool to have a dish of ice cream with his mother. As Sande and Kevin were enjoying their ice cream, a woman came in and sat down nearby. She ordered a cup of coffee and some ice cream and then lit up a cigarette. The cigarette smoke started to drift directly across the faces of Kevin and my wife. Most adults who are nonsmokers are familiar with this kind of agony in a restaurant or another public place. They usually persevere in silence, but not Kevin. Kevin looked at the woman indignantly and said, "Lady, *your* smoke is getting on *my* ice cream!"

My wife cringed and blushed. The offending woman crushed out her cigarette, muttered a hasty apology, and beat an even hastier retreat.

There's little doubt that when given any kind of opportunity, children are totally honest. And yet many times I see parents trying to beat or talk that honesty out of their children. I believe this is a tragic mistake. Parents should do everything possible to nurture honesty in their children. And the best way to teach honesty is to be honest. I urge parents to be as direct and honest with their children as possible, starting when they are very young. For some reason, we don't think children can handle the truth. We tend to "cover" when we talk with them. We don't tell them everything that goes on because we feel they are "too young to understand." I realize that restraint is needed in some situations, but I usually encourage parents to share their real feelings, problems, and concerns.

Some parents aren't sure about my advice. Won't fears and anxieties cause the child to be fearful and anxious? Well, yes, that is a possibility, if that is all you do and you are overdramatic in the bargain. But every parent can share bits and pieces of what is really going on—the fears, anxieties, and worries. As you share your real self, your children will begin to develop an appreciation for the fact that you are not some kind of machine. They will learn that you are a real person who has feelings and needs and, yes, even failures. In short, the child will learn that you are a lot like he is. The child will say to himself, *Mommy knows what it is like to be afraid and to be worried. She understands when I am afraid and worried.*

All this may sound a bit scary to some parents who have been trained to always look as if they are in control and "competent." But I am convinced that it is important for our children to see us as imperfect—yes, and even "crummy"— in the truest sense of these words. In my opinion, there is no better way to teach a child about having true faith in God. When the child learns that his parents are truly dependent upon the grace of God and that they need God's help, he will see that God is very real and not just a "belief" that is talked about in an abstract way. I always suggest that parents pray with their children as they take time to share their heartfelt thoughts and feelings. Prayer is a wonderful way to communicate with your child about the realities of life.

Being this kind of honest role model may sound a bit daring, but I believe it's well worth the risk. Here are some reasons:

1. *Through your honesty children learn that it's okay to be less than perfect.* Having faults, worries, and failures does not make a person weird or inferior. On the contrary, it is

the strong person who can admit his weaknesses.

2. *As you model honesty before your child, you have tremendous opportunities to build intimacy and a strong parent-child relationship.* By being honest, you invite the child into your confidence, into your private world where few people outside the family ever have a chance to observe or listen in. In effect, you say to the child, "I trust you. I value your opinion. I know you are a capable person."

3. *As you model honesty you have opportunities to share your faith in God with your child.* You don't have to simply talk about praying to God and trusting God. You can invite your child to actually do these things with you. There is no better approach to reality than that.

Parents Need a Game Plan

Obviously, children learn in many other ways besides the three we've looked at in this chapter. But I have highlighted birth order, purposive behavior, and modeling to emphasize the importance of realizing that your children are individuals and each of them tests and discovers and learns through his own particular eyes. Reality Discipline is based on understanding the uniqueness in each child, but Reality Discipline is no magic panacea. You don't repeat the term six times over the child and expect miraculous results every time. Reality Discipline is something that must be practiced by both parents in a consistent and coordinated way. If only one parent is trying to use Reality Discipline, the results will be negligible. Some anonymous, wise sage has observed that you can fool an adult, but you can't fool a child. After counseling thousands of children and their parents, I agree totally. Children are so very perceptive. If they see Mom practicing one philosophy of discipline and Dad another, they will do everything that they can to play one parent against the other.

As a family psychologist, I have a basic love for all children, but that love does not make me blind to reality. That's why I affectionately say, "Children are the enemy!" They act out of selfishness and concern for getting things their own way. If they see any light at all between Mom and Dad, they will find ingenious ways to drive a wedge between them. I warn parents to be on their guard or their children will make them do things or say things they will later regret.

Whenever possible, I urge a couple to do all in their power to come together and be one in their parenting. In Philippians 2:2 Paul urges all Christians to work together "... with one heart and mind and purpose" (TLB). Where could this advice be more needed than in the home and family? I believe it is critical that parents are in agreement while facing a child in a disciplinary situation. When parents disagree, it should be thoroughly "hashed out" behind closed doors. Talk it through and then when you come out and talk to your children and make remarks and decisions that affect their lives, they will see you working together in concert, not in disharmony.

A family lives together, but each member learns individually. Each of your children perceives reality through eyes that are unique. The child born first sees things from a much different perspective from the child born last. The child born in the middle has still another view that is especially his. Wherever they land on that birth-order ladder, you can be sure your children will be testing, probing, and using all the powers at their disposal to gain as much control as they can. And their eyes are always watching. What do they see in your home? What they see is what they will learn.

3

Why Reward and Punishment Don't Work

Most of us who grew up in traditional homes experienced the two most common methods of controlling a child's behavior: reward and punishment. Both are used on people of all ages and positions in our society. Reward has long been a standby to get others to behave the way we want them to. If we can't get their cooperation through reward, we use punishment.

Why the System Isn't Working

Some parenting theories claim that if you reward positive behavior and punish negative behavior, children are quick to catch on and soon become little angels. Many parents have tied right into this basic system of reward and punishment. But in my counseling practice, I see examples every week of why the system just isn't working. Reward and punishment may have been effective in past generations, but it doesn't take a psychologist to see that the theory is having problems in the 1980s.

There are several basic reasons for this. Perhaps the key reason is the strong emphasis on democracy in our present society. As soon as they are able to comprehend, children start to pick up the idea that they are equal to everyone else—including adults. From preschool through high school and college children are taught that they have been "created equal" and that they have a right to speak up. They have even decided they can "demand their rights." There have been court cases in which children have actually sued their parents for various reasons. Not only that—they won!

Obviously, there is a good side to all of this democratic teaching. God has created everyone as individuals. Certainly He loves each person equally despite size or age. Every one of us is endowed with "certain inalienable rights" by our Creator.

But the bad side crops up when children start believing they have as much authority as adults and don't need to listen to adult authority. In many school systems teachers despair because of discipline problems. And where do the discipline problems start? They start at home, where Mom and Dad have already given up and allowed little Festus to rule the roost.

In order for reward and punishment to be effective, the people receiving those rewards and punishments need to buy into the system. Parents and schoolteachers still use reward and punishment and will continue to do so, but the problem is the children aren't buying the way they used to. They may go along with the whole thing, but it really isn't helping them develop and grow into mature persons.

If reward and punishment no longer really work as effective disciplinary tools, what should take their place? I believe we find the answer in Ephesians 6:4, TLB, which talks about "loving discipline." The Apostle Paul cautioned parents to not bring up their children in a way that would cause resentment and feelings of anger (which is exactly what reward and punishment accomplishes). Instead parents are to develop skills that focus on two other techniques. The answer to reward and punishment is loving discipline and encouragement.

Try Encouragement Instead of Reward

There is a subtle but important difference between encouragement and reward. Granted, reward works with young children. Tell the typical three-year-old you will give him a lollipop if he does what you ask and he will cooperate! Tell your twelve-year-old you will pay him five dollars for cleaning up the backyard and chances are your twelve-year-old will do the job. But sooner or later, every parent has the same question: Do I want my children to do things in the home for rewards? For example, why should my twelve-year-old clean the backyard?

1. He is a member of the household.
2. Cleaning the yard is a job that has to be done.
3. He will be paid five dollars for his trouble.
4. I want him to become involved in the family and feel a responsibility toward helping it function.

Obviously cleaning the backyard to pick up a five-dollar bill is a much different motivation from the other three. After all, it isn't just Mom and Dad's home, it's the entire family's home. They *all* live there. When it comes to doing things around the home, it's preferable that the motivation come from within, and I do not mean from within the pocketbook. The trouble with a reward system is that motivation always comes from without. If a reward system is the chief way you have of motivating your children, you are in danger of creating "carrot seekers" who are always looking for a reward (carrot) every time they do something right, good, or noteworthy in life.

To illustrate just how this works let's go back to the illustration of twelve-year-old Harold and the five-dollar "carrot" he was offered for cleaning the backyard. Harold goes out and accomplishes the task in good style and is paid his five dollars. Mom is happy because the backyard is clean and Harold is happy because he's five dollars richer. End of problem, right? Wrong! About seven days later Harold goes out, cleans up the backyard again, and asks, "Mom, where's my five dollars?"

Mom looks a bit puzzled and says, "Harold, I'm not quite sure what you're talking about. What do you mean, honey?"

"Well, Mom, last week you gave me five dollars for cleaning up the backyard and so I cleaned up the backyard again today. I'd like to have my five dollars."

You may have had a similar situation in your own home. The point is rather obvious. Once we start paying children for tasks they should be doing simply because they are part of the family, we can soon find ourselves riding a tiger. And as someone once pointed out, "He who rides a twelve-year-old tiger finds it difficult to get off."

I'm not saying that there aren't legitimate cases where you might want to arrange a special project for which your child might be paid, but the far more common syndrome that I see in my counseling work is that parents will often get suckered into having to pay their children for just about everything they do around the home. If you are slipping into this kind of trap, now is the time to put a stop to it and have a talk about being willing to develop a life-style that centers more on self-discipline, humility, and good works without always expecting recognition in the form of cold, hard cash.

Encouragement Emphasizes the Act

There is a subtle distinction between reward and encouragement. A lot of that subtle distinction is in the attitude of the parent and the basic guidelines the parent is laying down in the family. Let's go back to our illustration of Harold in the backyard for just another minute. In a home that was trying to stress encouragement rather than reward, how would Mom react to her twelve-year-old after he had cleaned up the backyard? First of all, she would not have dangled a carrot. She would simply have asked him to clean up the backyard because it needed to be done. Then suppose

Harold did it, and did it quite well. What would Mom do and say?

I think an encouraging approach would go something like this: "Harold, what a fine job. I'll bet you're proud of yourself. That must have taken a lot of work! Gee, the yard looks really great. I appreciate your work so much. Thanks, honey."

Let's take another look at those words. Note that the emphasis is on the act and not on Harold. Mom does not say, "My, you're a good boy because you cleaned up the backyard so nicely." It's always a good idea to avoid associating a child's "goodness" with how well he does a certain task. Suppose Harold had done a rather slipshod piece of work on the backyard (a quite possible occurrence with many twelve-year-old boys). But if Harold had done a poor job, that would not make him "bad." What Mom would have to do is deal with the fact that the backyard was not acceptable. She would have to try to encourage Harold to do a better job.

In our example, however, Harold does do a fine job and so Mom can tell him so. But she never links his goodness or worth as a person to what he has done. She thanks him, appreciates the work, and observes that the yard really looks great. And in this subtle way, she encourages Harold to do other jobs well, simply for the satisfaction and not for money or for some kind of label that tells him he is good and worthwhile.

What I'm trying to get at here is that we must do everything we can to encourage our children and help them see they are not loved only when they perform correctly. Love and approval based on performance is conditional. Reality Discipline always seeks to love the child *unconditionally.* Our ultimate example is God Himself, who loves us unconditionally with an unqualified love. We can always come to Him, even when we have botched it. Perhaps the greater truth is that we can come to Him *especially* when we have botched it.

In a home where encouragement and unconditional love are the real goals, the child experiences words and actions that say, "Hey, I love you—no matter what! I may not always like things you do or say, but my love for you never ends." That kind of approach is much different from the one that says, "I love you if. . . ." or, "I love you when. . . ." In other words, Mom will love Harold *if* he cleans up the backyard nicely. Mom will love Harold *when* he cleans up the backyard.

As Josh McDowell points out in his fine book *Givers, Takers and Other Kinds of Lovers,* loving your children if and when is not the answer. McDowell observes that the only real way to love is to simply say, "I love you." There are no ifs, or whens, or ands, or buts. You simply communicate in every way you can to your child, "I love you." Our children need to know they are loved absolutely, regardless of how they perform in different areas of their lives.

Remember that the key difference between reward and encouragement is that the reward is centered on the child himself.

"My, you're really a good boy for doing the dishes. Here's a quarter."

"My, you're a good boy for cleaning up your room. You can stay up until ten o'clock."

Statements like the above only program the child to believe he is loved *because* he does certain things. Avoid that kind of nonsense at all costs. Instead, use encouragement which zeros in on your child's behavior. As you respond positively to your child's behavior, he will feel unconditionally loved and approved.

Real Discipline Is Not Punishment

While it is difficult to distinguish between reward and encouragement, I think it is even harder to separate discipline from punishment. Like reward, punishment focuses on the child. And like encouragement, discipline focuses on the *behavior* of the child.

Ephesians 6:4, TLB, tells us to bring our children up "with the loving discipline the Lord himself approves." But just what does *loving discipline* mean? The words almost seem to contradict each other. We want to communicate love to our child, yet there are times when we have to discipline him or her. I believe the two words do go together and make sense, *if* we understand what real discipline is. I have found there are many ways to discipline a child. These methods make sense, are direct and swift, and they are action-oriented. Most important, they produce far better results than traditional punishment.

For example, Mother is on the telephone and her six-year-old starts acting up. He's loud, cranky, and is really going out of his way to make Mom's telephone conversation miserable, if not impossible. Mom chooses to ignore it and this lasts for a few minutes. Suddenly she blows her cool.

"Excuse me, Marge," she says. "I have a problem." Mom grabs her six-year-old by the neck, whacks him a few good ones, and jerks him by the arm into his room, saying, "Now, you just sit there until you can learn some manners!"

Well, what has really happened during this rather familiar scene? Mom has tried to be patient but she lost her cool and control. She wound up lashing out to punish her child who is now bitter, angry, and resentful. How could we rewrite the scenario to have Mom discipline her six-year-old, rather than punish him? How could we make the discipline realistic and effective?

Let's go back to the first moment the six-year-old started disturbing Mom's conversation on the telephone. It was *then* that she should have acted quickly and decisively. She could have said, "Excuse me, Marge, I have to talk to Billy for a minute."

Then Mom could have taken six-year-old Billy firmly, but not harshly, and led him off to another room in the house or possibly outside the house to the backyard. By doing this she would have demonstrated that Billy could continue his behavior but he no longer had the right to do it where he was going to interrupt Mom's right to talk on the telephone. Mom could have conveyed this to him by simply saying: "I'm talking on the telephone and I don't want to be interrupted. Now you play by yourself and as soon as I'm through I'll come and tell you, and if you need anything I'll try to help you."

But notice, there would be no hitting and Mom would be in control of her emotions. And all the while Billy would be getting discipline instead of punishment. And it would be the right kind of discipline. One thing I've learned about six-year-olds is that they don't like to be isolated. They want to hear *everything* that is going on. But for the attention-getting child who just has to keep bugging Mom or Dad while they are on the telephone, isolation is a very, very good *disciplinary* measure.

Why Punishment Doesn't Work

As I have parented my own children and counseled many parents about their offspring, I have learned that discipline beats punishment every time. If punishment worked, it wouldn't be necessary to ever punish a child more than once for any infraction of the rules. If punishment really worked, the child would learn his lesson the first time around. But punishment *doesn't* work. It seems to work—for the moment—but essentially thoughts are gathering in the child's mind that run something like this: *All right, Mom, you win this round, but I'll get even. I'm gonna get you back!*

Punishment teaches children that because we—their parents—are bigger and stronger, we can push them around. We can force our will upon them. And because we—the parents—can get away with this, it reinforces the idea in our own minds that it's perfectly all right to force our will upon our children. After all, we are their parents. With Christian parents the problem is still more serious. We always go to our old favorite, "Children, obey your parents," to justify our heavy-handed tactics. But forcing your will upon your children just isn't scriptural. We have already talked about the real meaning of the word *rod* in Scripture and how people not only misquote Scripture ("Spare the rod and spoil the child") but also misuse the entire idea of what the biblical writers meant when they talked about the rod. (See chapter 1.)

You can find no better model for discipline than Jesus Himself during His ministry on earth. The Lord never beat His disciples over the head. He always dealt with them directly, fairly, and firmly. He never screamed and hollered; He never gave evasive answers. But He always gave His disciples a choice. He let them learn to be responsible and to choose for themselves. Jesus was the model teacher of Reality Discipline.

Granted, Jesus was dealing with adults and we are talking about disciplining children. Nonetheless, the principles are still the same. Disciplining children is difficult and it does take some skills. That's one of the basic reasons I've written this book. I want to help parents learn skills and ways of disciplining their children in all kinds of situations. I want to help parents to communicate respect to children while at the same time teaching their children to respect them. Parents should always try to act in a way that enhances their child's ability to respect and honor them. Why? Because it not only builds the family but it strengthens the very fabric of society as well.

I have yet to find the Bible teaching any principle that does not build people and the societies in which they live, if they are interested at all in living correctly. The Fifth Commandment clearly states: "Honor your father and your mother, so that you may live long in the land. . ." (Exodus 20:12, NIV). And Paul echoed the commandment's teaching when he said, "Children, obey your parents in the Lord, for this is right. 'Honor your father and mother'—which is the first commandment with a promise—'that it may go well

with you and that you may enjoy long life on the earth.' "
(Ephesians 6:1–3, NIV).

Clearly, God's Word has set up Christian parents with a
practical and sound system. When they work the system
correctly, everybody lives a longer and happier life. When
the system is neglected or ignored through extremes like authoritarianism or permissiveness, things do not go well.

One of the basic reasons punishment does not work in the
long run is that God did not plan for the use of punishment
in a family. When God refers to His own children (believ-
ers), He talks about chastisement, chastening, or discipline.
(See, for example, Hebrews 12:5–11.) Since God created us
He knows what works best with us and for us. What works
best is the kind of discipline that trains and teaches in a
way the Lord Himself would approve.

Training Up a Child Takes Time

Proverbs 22:6, NIV, reminds us, "Train a child in the way
he should go, and when he is old he will not turn from it."
Training up a child means putting time and energy into
teaching the child acceptable behavior in any number of social situations. But the bottom line is what the child does
when the parents aren't there. What makes a child obey
when Mom or Dad isn't around to crack down? Perhaps it's
fear of punishment; perhaps it's the child's conscience.

I believe that as you train up your child with loving discipline, his conscience is developed in such a way that he is
much more likely to behave properly when you aren't there.
But to train him properly you must use encouragement and
discipline, not reward and punishment. Parents who use reward and punishment as the two principal motivators of
their children's behavior are not really helping them develop a good conscience. Instead, the children learn, "I'll be
good when Mom and Dad are around, but as soon as they're
out of sight, I'll do what I want."

Using Reality Discipline in a loving way won't guarantee

that your children will always be perfect little angels, but I can guarantee that it will breed more honesty and communication between the two of you.

The best way to develop a sound conscience in your child is to teach him or her accountability. You teach accountability by setting the guidelines—the rules, if you please. The guidelines set the limits and it's important that your children understand what the limits are and why they are there. It's up to us, the parents, to discipline our children swiftly and quietly, while being open to discuss the "whys and wherefores" in a particular situation.

Another important developer of the conscience is the concept of forgiveness. We must be able to teach our children forgiveness and give them opportunities to express their remorse for violations of the family guidelines. And we must be able to express remorse ourselves. The only way we can ever teach a child to say, "I'm sorry," is for him to hear it from our lips first. Parents always train up their children in the way they should go by example. Believe me, the old cliché is true: children pay much more attention to our actions than they do to our words.

Proverbs 22:6 contains still another truth for training up children. The more correct Hebrew translation of the verse is, "Train up a child in his own way. . . ." This doesn't mean you let the child have his way and let him do whatever he wants (permissiveness). What it does mean is that every child is different. As we saw in chapter 2, every child sees the world through his own unique eyes. He has a certain temperament, a certain way of reacting to situations, a certain kind of personality.

When we talk about disciplining our children, we must keep in mind that each of God's creatures is created differently. No two of us are the same. I'm not naive enough to think any one method of discipline can work with every child. Because some children are more strong-willed and have a higher activity level, they will need one kind of disciplinary measure in a given situation, while another child who is more passive can be disciplined in a totally different way. Training up a child in his own way means being willing to show each child that you realize he is an individual and that each situation needs to be handled according to his needs and temperament. Reality Discipline is a system that gives you the kind of latitude you need to train your children in the way that is best for them. Each child is unique. Resist the temptation to compare your son or daughter with others.

From Allowance to Accountability

Training children to be accountable and responsible not only takes time; it also takes strategy. One of the best strategies I know is in the use of the allowance to help children become accountable and responsible. Now, the allowance is obviously not a new invention. But how the allowance is used and how it is given can make a vast difference in the behavior of your children. I suggest to the families I counsel that each child in the family get a different amount of money for his allowance (unless, of course, you have a set of twins). Age is as good a criterion as any on which to base the amount of an allowance, and it is logical that the older the child, the more his allowance should be.

I also recommend that the allowance be seen as part of the family budget. An allowance is something each child should have, just as Dad or Mom has lunch money each week. The allowance is a practical and effective way to give children the opportunity to begin to manage money, and at the same time it gives them a feeling of positive self-worth. It never hurts your self-esteem—whether you're six or sixty—to feel a jingle in your pocket that says, "Hey, I have some money of my own!"

Another obvious rule that most parents understand about the allowance is that it should come to each child on a particular day each week or month. It should be something children can look foward to on a regular basis.

I have found, however, that one thing some parents fail to understand is that an allowance is something each child should be able to spend as he or she sees fit. To give that child an allowance and then turn around and tell him how to spend it is to go right back to the problem of authoritarianism that I discussed in the previous chapters. The authoritarian makes all decisions for his child—including how the child should spend his allowance. The child learns nothing about handling money or accountability. To teach a child to be accountable and responsible, you have to create an environment in which he feels that it is safe to test and discover and learn. And he will have to learn some things the hard way. An allowance is a great tool to let him do just that.

Whenever I talk about allowances I always talk about responsibilities. Since a child is a responsible member of the household, he should get an allowance. And, because he is a responsible member of the family, he should also have certain responsibilities or chores. You can decide on these chores at family meetings at the dinner table or during other special times. The parents should be careful, however, to not make the allowance equivalent to "pay" for doing chores. The child should understand, though, that he has responsibilities. He should know that he will get his allowance simply because he is a member of the family. Nonetheless, an allowance is not completely without conditions. As a responsible member of the family, each child does have chores to help the family run more smoothly.

While I believe a child should be able to spend his allowance as he or she sees fit, the allowance can also be used as an opportunity to teach saving and stewardship. In our home, we give the child the opportunity to choose to save some of his money. When a child wants to put some of his money in the bank, I match that money dollar for dollar. We also have taught each of our children the importance of giving some of our money back to God. We try to help our children see that ideally some of their allowance should be given to God, some should be saved, and the rest can be spent as the child sees fit.

So, how does the allowance become a tool for teaching accountability and responsibility? Very simply. Suppose a child takes his allowance of one dollar (or whatever the amount might be) and blows it all on candy. And, for good measure, let's suppose that the child buys the candy while he's accompanying Mom to the supermarket. Now, remember the rule: give some to God, save some, and spend the rest as you see fit. It will take real discipline on your part to let the child buy seventy or eighty cents worth of candy and eat it. I'm not suggesting that you would allow this to go on week after week because more is involved than spending the allowance; health and nutrition are important, too. But I believe it would be worthwhile to let the child blow his allowance for at least a few weeks in this fashion. In that way, through his own experience, he will learn that it is foolish to be extravagant and to waste his money for the entire week on candy the very first day. Invariably, during that same week, the child is going to want something else, but he won't have any money, and this is where the parents have a beautiful opportunity to let reality be the teacher and disciplinarian.

There you are a few days later, in another supermarket, and your child says, "Mommy, can I have this sugarless gum?" You look the child right in the eye and say, "Harold, of course you can. Just use your allowance."

But Harold looks up sheepishly and says, "But Mom, I spent all my allowance last Monday."

"Well, honey," you say, "put it back and we'll see you on Saturday. You can buy the gum then when you get your new allowance."

The above example illustrates why I believe the allowance is such a strategic tool in teaching accountability. The allowance is a perfect way to train your children to learn to make intelligent decisions on a daily basis. After a few negative experiences, most children learn not to spend carelessly all at once. Some of them even begin to learn to tuck away some money for the proverbial rainy day.

How to Get Those Chores Done

Don't fail to see the strategic connection between allowances and the assignment of chores or responsibilities to each child. Every child ought to have some responsibility in the home just as soon as possible. Even a three-year-old can help set the table. True, it might look like a three-year-old set it, but it is important to give each child the opportunity to take part.

But once we assign responsibilities to everyone, we face the time-honored bugaboo. What happens when the children don't meet their responsibilities, when they don't do their chores? In traditional homes, where reward and punishment flourish, Mom gets on the child's case. She yells and screams until the chore gets done. If necessary, stronger measures are used: grounding, being sent to bed without supper, and even spanking. But in a home using Reality Discipline, encouragement and discipline are the order of the day. When a child doesn't do his chores by the predetermined time, Mom and Dad move in swiftly and calmly to deal with the situation. As managers and leaders in the home, Mom and Dad have to decide what to do. One option is that they can hire someone else to do the job for the child. For example, if little Harold doesn't take the garbage out, perhaps his sister will. Is this imposing on little sister? Hardly. Little sister gets part of Harold's allowance for her trouble!

Notice how Reality Discipline works in this case. Harold loses some of his allowance, but you haven't taken it away from him to "punish" him. Essentially, he has paid money back into the family budget to have someone else take care of his responsibility. Harold may see this as punishment, so you must remain firm and gentle as you explain that punishment is not involved. There is only so much money in the family budget, and when someone else must be hired, Harold must contribute part of his allowance to get the work done. If Harold is on the ball at all, he will soon learn that losing money due to forgetfulness, sloppiness, or rebelliousness is not a very wise choice. Not only that, but he will see his money going to his brother or sister and that will *really* hurt. Chances are good to excellent that Harold will make some drastic changes in his behavior and that he will get his chores completed on time.

Hiring little sister is a perfect way to let reality be the teacher in this case. Isn't this just like the realities of everyday life? If Dad and Mom don't go to work, they don't get paid. It's as simple as that.

I am convinced that the training ground for life ought to be the home. We need to begin to hold children accountable for their decisions. In too many homes this isn't happening. Mom and Dad are always available to remind, coax, bribe, and push. Yes, maybe the chores do get done—eventually— but at what price? Part of that price is that Mom and Dad have to constantly nag the children, which Ephesians 6:4 clearly warns us not to do. But even more damaging is that through their constant nagging, coaxing, and bribing, parents are teaching their children that when they grow up and get out into life there will always be somebody there to push, motivate, and reward them for their behavior. But of course, life isn't like that. We can give our children a great tool for living by teaching them to be accountable and responsible. As the old saying puts it, teach them to stand on their own two feet.

Variety Is the Spice of Responsibility

Before leaving the topic of chores and responsibilities, we should take a good look at the concept of variety. The bad news about chores is that they have to be done; the good news is that they can change. Buford doesn't have to look forward to being the "garbage man" for life. The job can be passed down to a younger brother or sister as he grows older.

In fact, I surprise a lot of parents with my recommendation to give their older children *less* to do. My reasoning is this: I believe that as a child grows older and gets into high school he faces much more pressure by way of academic challenges and extracurricular activities. I believe the high schooler's chores in the home should decrease and that the younger children in the family should take up the slack. For many families I know, the reverse seems to be true. The older children are saddled with responsibilities and they continue to be responsible year in and year out while their younger siblings get off with less to do.

If you have children from teens down to younger years, think about it for a moment. What responsibilities did your sixteen-year-old son have when he was ten? Compare those responsibilities with your ten-year-old daughter's responsibilities today. In your family the responsibility level may come out even, but in many families I counsel I find that the sixteen-year-old had more responsibilities when he was ten than does his ten-year-old sister today.

The challenge for parents is to keep moving responsibilities downward in the family and to be ever aware that the younger children should have the opportunity to pitch in on an equal basis.

In fact, as I said, if at all possible teenagers should be given fewer chores in order to free them for studies, extracurricular activities, athletics, and all the other pressures that come their way in high school. I'm not saying that teenagers should be allowed to sit back and do nothing while their younger brothers and sisters are doing all the work around the house. And it may not be possible to relieve teenagers of certain chores. Perhaps they don't have a younger brother or sister who could step in at that particular point, or there may be some other problem. The rule of thumb that I always urge parents to seek, however, is to spread the responsibilities around and try to relieve the teenagers in the family of as much pressure as possible while helping the younger children learn accountability and responsibility at their end.

Naturally, once the teenager is relieved of some of the chores and responsibilities, he then has to be accountable for how he uses his time. Goofing off, not studying, and just hanging around and getting into trouble are all unacceptable ways to use free time. Talk with your teenager about his responsibilities. Explain that you have tried to lighten the load at home so that he can meet the heavier responsibilities at school.

It's Never Too Late to Start

On the other hand, you may be wondering why I am making so much out of assigning responsibilities and chores. In many homes today, in suburban America in particular, finding chores for children is almost a lost art. Many adults can remember how they grew up in rural settings where they experienced definite responsibilities. Chores they had to do made a noticeable impact on the well-being and even the income of a family. Today, however, we have moved in the other direction, toward being sophisticated and soft. It's easier to hire a gardener than hassle Johnny about mowing the lawn. In the interest of time or convenience, we fail to provide our children with opportunities to become accountable and responsible in the home by meeting certain definite responsibilities daily or weekly. I believe that a major challenge for parents today is to always be seeking ways to divide responsibility among family members in a fair way. The responsibilities may vary and they can change from time to time (for example, when children become teenagers) but everyone should have something for which he is accountable.

If you believe you may fall into the category of parents who haven't done as much as they could to give their children opportunities to be accountable through family responsibilities and chores, it's never too late to start. But I suggest you start in a low-key manner. Sit down and talk with your children and allow them to pick and choose what their responsibilities might be. List all the jobs that need to be done. The entire family could help identify what all these jobs are. Write all the jobs down and then assign various tasks. Try to allow the children to choose their tasks, but if there is squabbling or bickering, you may just have to arbitrarily assign certain duties with the comment, "Let's try it this way and see how it works." Keep reminding your children that being assigned a chore is not a life sentence. Keep the entire situation flexible. Remember that what you are really after with the assignment of responsibilities is to teach your children to be accountable and responsible.

I have talked a lot about accountability and responsibility in this chapter. We have looked at the difference between encouragement and reward as well as the difference between punishment and discipline. Perhaps we need to look further at just how Reality Discipline works when children don't come through. What happens when they don't cooperate? I have a favorite little saying that I use in my seminars: "Sometimes you have to pull the rug out and let the little buzzards tumble."

Parents usually chuckle as they picture their "little buzzards" tumbling about. Of course, I caution them that whenever you "pull the rug" on a child you do it in a way that teaches him and doesn't hurt him. In the next chapter, we'll take a detailed look at just how to pull the rug.

4

"Pull the Rug Out and Let the Little Buzzards Tumble"

Someone said it: "Actions speak louder than words."

Like all true sayings, this one has become a cliché, but it remains as true as ever, especially in regard to child rearing. Our kids do pay attention to what we do, and they don't always pay attention to what we say.

That's why I coined that little saying that I use constantly in seminars and counseling sessions: "Sometimes you have to pull the rug out and let the little buzzards tumble."

If you're a mom, you may shudder a bit at my referring to your gift from God as a "little buzzard." And perhaps "pulling the rug out" sounds more like punishment (maybe mayhem) than discipline. Please bear with me. I'm from Tucson and here in Arizona we like to think "little buzzards" are cute—especially the ones who roost on our backyard swing sets. As for "pulling the rug out" being punishment and mayhem, not so. To pull out the rug is the key to making Reality Discipline work. Let me show you why.

A couple of years ago I worked in counseling with Paul, age ten. He lived in a rural community and liked animals a great deal. Without his parents' permission, he bought (with his own money) two baby pigs from another boy. Paul brought his pigs home and showed them to Mom. Mom wasn't ready for baby pigs and told him he would have to get rid of the little porkers; they simply couldn't stay. Two weeks later, however, the pigs were still there. Paul had used all the tricks on his parents: he had already spent his money; he couldn't take them back; he would take good care of them and raise them up, sell them, and even make some money, and so on.

But Paul's mother simply couldn't agree to having those pigs around. Paul stubbornly insisted on being granted the privilege of keeping his pigs. The whole thing was turning into something of a family pork-barrel scandal when the parents sought me out as counsel.

My recommendation was swift and brief: get rid of the pigs. Their response beautifully illustrates the dilemma parents find themselves in when they're not willing to pull the rug out. How could they get rid of the pigs when they belonged to Paul, they wanted to know. And where could they take them?

I challenged Paul's parents with the thought that their child had been irresponsible when he brought home two animals to the family farm without the consent of his parents. I reminded them that as Paul's parents they were in authority over him. When a child steps over the line and by his actions says, "You're not my authority—I'll do my own thing," parents have the responsibility to act quickly and decisively—and pull the rug out.

Paul's parents got the message and they got rid of the pigs. In fact, they got rid of them rather easily by finding another family who was willing to take them—without having to pay for them. Of course, Paul wasn't very happy. He lost all the money it cost him to buy the two pigs. And that just might have been the best discipline in the whole affair. It was a consequence his parents had to let happen.

When Paul came home and discovered his pigs were gone, he was outraged. In fact, he was beside himself. But his parents told me later that this "rug-pulling incident" with the pigs really got Paul's attention. It led to some positive changes in his behavior.

As I'm sure you have already suspected, the pig incident wasn't an isolated case in Paul's life. He had already been trying to prove he could "do his own thing" in many different ways. Still, it wasn't easy for Paul's parents to see him lose the money he had worked so hard to earn by doing chores on another farm. Nonetheless, it was a great lesson and he learned it the hard way. Mom and Dad had been very patient during the two weeks they had reminded and coaxed him to get rid of the pigs. There was a good possibility he could have taken them back to the farm where he had bought them. His friend may even have given the money back. But Paul was so determined to do his own thing that he didn't bother to try, and he paid the price.

As distasteful as pulling the rug out from under Paul was, it was still the best discipline (and love) his parents could possibly demonstrate. My counseling and speaking in seminars across the country has convinced me that parents have been sold a bill of goods. They have heard that psychologists believe a child's psyche is so very fragile that we shouldn't hurt or upset the child in any way. I agree with Ephesians 6:4. We shouldn't frustrate our kids or "provoke them to wrath" (see KJV). But to say they are too delicate to learn from discipline based on love and reality is foolish.

As I mentioned in an earlier chapter, children will constantly test their parents. They don't test us out of pure orneriness; what they really want to know is whether or not we care. When we are firm and prove that we do care, they may not like it but they do respect us and appreciate us. Let me repeat that "firm" discipline is not punishment. In this particular situation with Paul and his pigs, the loss of his money (not to mention the loss of the pigs) provided a perfect form of discipline. What would have been inappropriate—and probably of little effect—would have been screaming, name-calling, or spanking. And right here is as good a point as any to talk about that most traditional form of "discipline" of them all: corporal punishment. You may have been wondering whether I believed in it or not. Read on.

Does Pulling the Rug Out Ever Include the Paddle?

Yes, I believe that spanking does fit into my rug-pulling philosophy. But spanking has to be used in the appropriate situation. For example, a swat on the bottom can be a very good disciplinary measure for a young child in the two- to seven-year-old range when he is being absolutely willful and rebellious.

Go easy, however, on swatting children under two years of age. I believe children eighteen months and younger should never be swatted. A child that young doesn't understand what is happening. In fact, children under eighteen months do not have complete conceptual development. *No* is not a word they really understand. (Yes, I know they seem to, but what they are understanding far better is the look on your face.) When you say, "Come here," to an eighteen-month-old, it is usually an effective way to get him to run in the other direction. Children at this stage are "oppositional." That is, they often want to do the opposite of what you suggest. Holding out a toy or the child's "blankie" is a much more appropriate means to get the child to come to you.

As children reach the age of two, they are more capable of conceptualizing. They are also getting past the oppositional stage. Many mothers would disagree with me there because everyone is familiar with the "terrible twos" syndrome. Nonetheless, at two and above, most children can understand a request such as, "Come here," but they may be defiant and refuse to come. We are all familiar with those times when children do force us into a showdown. In situations where it's a case of Dad or Mom winning or Festus winning, my money is on Dad and Mom every time. If a swat is necessary, so be it. The reality that I've seen in family after family is that if little Festus wins, the game is over and discipline is down the drain.

The Right and Wrong Way to Spank

There is, however, the right and wrong way to spank. Entire books have been written on the subject, but here are some guidelines.

The key to spanking a child is being in control of your own emotions. While it seems a contradiction, spanking is something that must be done in love. True, you may not feel very "loving" while administering the spanking, but the way you show your love is by not losing your cool.

There is a world of difference between one or several good swats and beating on a child in absolute rage, which is usually accompanied by shouting and verbal abuse.

The second key principle to apply when spanking is what I call "follow-up time." Some writers on discipline and child rearing indicate that once the spanking has been administered, a child feels that he has paid his debt and therefore the situation has resolved itself and is over. I'm not comfortable with leaving it at that. I believe that when you spank a child, you have an obligation to tell the child exactly why he was spanked. You have the further obligation to listen to the child, and immediately after the spanking may be a good time for him to talk about his feelings: what made him angry, what made him say what he said or do what he did, and so on. The parent, as well as the child, can always learn from these situations. And it's even possible that the parent will learn that he acted in haste and perhaps spanked for the wrong reason. If that happens, the parent owes the child an apology and it should come immediately.

The key to follow-up, however, is physical contact. Hold the child and talk to him about your feelings. Explain why you were upset. Explain what made you angry and why it was necessary to spank. And explain what you expect from the child in the future.

It's quite possible the child may want to apologize or show remorse. He may say something like, "I'm sorry, Mommy." If he does, encourage him in a warm and loving manner. You may wish to say that you are sorry, too, but you had a responsibility to spank in order to teach him the right way.

Always try to reassure your child, particularly if he is between the ages of two and seven. During the "follow-up time," tell him you love him. Explain that there will be times when he will do things that are wrong, but even though he does these things you will never stop loving him and caring about him.

So much for some general rules for spanking. But a lot of parents want to know *when* they should spank and *why*. I believe that spanking is particularly helpful with young children when their safety is involved. For example, a two-and-a-half-year-old may repeatedly get too close to a swimming pool or some other dangerous area. If he willfully disobeys a mother's instructions, it can be very effective to give him a swat and move him to safer ground. If he repeats his violation, you may need to give him another swat and isolate him from the pool area by keeping him in the house.

The same principles hold true for children who constantly run toward the street and fail to obey Mother's admonitions to be careful. Some child-rearing specialists advise never to swat a child with your hand. They say to use a ruler or a paddle. I disagree with that approach. I believe that love and discipline go hand in hand (pun intended). Proverbs 13:24 says if you love your child you will discipline him. The same hand that guides a child across a busy street must sometimes discipline to help him learn. The key to spanking is to do it with love.

Be Sure They Feel Loved

Like any form of discipline, spanking is more effective when the child feels loved. I like the advice by Larry Tomczak in his book *God, the Rod, and Your Child's Bod* (published by Fleming H. Revell Company). I must confess, the title threw me at first, but Larry's approach to spanking as "the art of loving correction" is sound. Tomczak gives some practical suggestions for making a child feel loved. They include:

1. *Make sure you see your children as God sees them*—as a "gift," a "reward," and as "arrows"—not as an interruption, accident, or tax break (Psalms 127:3, 4, NAS).

2. *Cultivate a childlike attitude.* Don't take yourself too seriously. Rediscover play. Walk barefoot together across the wet grass. Ride a merry-go-round. Act out a story instead of merely reading it (Matthew 18:1–4).

3. *Give your children direct eye contact.* Jesus said that "the eye is the lamp of the body . . ." (Matthew 6:22). He calls us "the apple of his eye" (Deuteronomy 32:10). The Lord said ". . . I will counsel you with my eye upon you" (Psalms 32:8). A child has a critical need for focused attention which enables him to feel respected, important, and loved. "Daddy (or Mommy) really cares about me . . . what I say . . . what I do."

4. *Physically express your love.* Regular hugging, kissing, sitting close together, tousling hair, tickling, rubbing backs . . . putting an arm on the shoulder . . . are all absolutely essential to assure a child's emotional security and to nurture his self-esteem. They communicate this thought: "I like you and enjoy being with you." These are the building blocks of a strong, healthy love bond.

5. *Train yourself to be a good listener.* Listening requires discipline, especially with children who can tell you the same Winnie the Pooh story a hundred times. It involves the eyes, ears, mind, and heart. It means kneeling at times so as to be on their level and to communicate eye to eye. It's important that as parents we respond to our child's feelings—"Rejoice with those who rejoice, weep with those who weep" (Romans 12:15)—and not *regularly* interrupt them

or cut them off. Such statements as "Not now, I'm busy" or "Tell me later" say to a child: *I guess I'm not as important to Mommy and Daddy as other things are.*

6. *Spend . . . time together.* There simply is no substitute for regular, consistent time spent together doing ordinary things (eating, working, walking, praying, driving, swimming, shopping) or "making memories" by doing extraordinary things (visits to a zoo, pet shop, amusement park, or hospital; playing table games, attending a sandlot softball game; picnicking, camping, biking, hiking, building a model plane; sewing a doll's outfit; sight-seeing, visiting museums, visiting your nearby fire station, and taking them for a tour of where Dad works).

I especially like what Larry Tomczak says about listening and spending time. Spending time with your children does create great memories. A child's life is so pliable during the formative years. Do your best to give your child a great gift every day: *yourself!* And be sure to listen. All parents look back and realize how quickly time passes. Use your time wisely. Listen to your children when they are little. They are much more likely to talk to you when they are older!

Respect Is a Two-Way Street

Spanking is a possible option for disciplining your child, but always be sure you are doing it as loving correction, not in any way that rejects your child. As Larry Tomczak says, if you find it necessary to administer a swat, do it not to humiliate or embarrass or to be cruel and harsh.

While spanking is an option for discipline, I believe it seldom should be the first choice when deciding on the best way to "pull the rug out" in order to help your child learn. I think life's best teachers are experiences in reality. I'm not saying spanking isn't reality, but I am saying that reality includes so many other approaches to loving discipline.

For example, you can use the power of choice—that is,

you can give your children choices. Many hassles develop in families between parents and children because of power struggles. In any parent-child relationship, there are bound to be times when there is a conflict of wills. Mother says Betsy will wear a certain dress and Betsy says she won't. Mother says she will and Betsy firmly resists again. And the war is on.

How can this kind of struggle be avoided? How can Mom teach her daughter to respect parental wishes? The obvious answer is for Mom to try to show her daughter some respect as well. And how can Mom accomplish this without giving up all of her authority? One possibility is to separate the clothes in Betsy's closet: put clothes for play and school on one side and clothes for Sunday school, church, and special occasions on the other. Then Betsy can make a choice and feel that she has some control over her own life.

You can go still further with the clothes closet arrangement and possibly break the clothes for school into certain categories; and you may want to put clothes for play in still another section.

As you make changes in a child's wardrobe, depending on the season, you can glean out clothes that no longer fit or that are inappropriate for one reason or another. You may want to involve your child in the gleaning-out process.

Through all of these simple actions, you will be allowing your child to make more and more decisions for herself. To be able to make some decisions for herself builds self-esteem and confidence. The child feels respected and will in turn be more likely to respect the parent. I have found it interesting that when a parent gives a certain amount of freedom to a child regarding choice of what the child might wear, the child often comes out dressed and asks for Mom's or Dad's approval concerning what he or she has on. This is just one simple example of a basic principle: if we do our job as parents and use our authority wisely, our children will respect us and our opinions.

Don't Demand Respect—Earn It

Granted, however, you don't gain your child's respect by using one simple strategy such as giving choices concerning what dress to wear. Like most important things in life, respect is not something you obtain easily. And another thing that parents—especially Christian parents—need to realize is that they can't *demand* respect from their children. Oh, I suppose you can demand it and all the while be pointing at Ephesians chapter 6, which clearly states that children are to respect their parents. But that may not cut much ice with little Snookie or Cletus. The way to gain respect from another person (and it helps to remember that our children *are* persons) is to earn that respect. Respect isn't like instant Jell-O pudding—it takes time to develop.

I remember going to the hospital to visit a fifteen-year-old girl who had tried to commit suicide. Her family contacted me immediately and asked me to pay her a visit. I cleared my schedule and went right to the hospital and as I was walking up to her room, the questions flooded my mind: Why would this girl want to take her life? What kind of predicaments and problems did she face?

When I got to her room I found a very beautiful teenager who was completely distraught, in tears and total depression. I asked her if she knew who I was and she said, "Yes."

I sat next to her, beside her bed, and simply asked, "Do you want to talk about it?"

She didn't answer. Instead she stared at the ceiling and the look on her face said quite plainly: "No, I *don't* want to talk about it."

I sensed that she was testing me to see whether I really cared about her or whether I had been sent by her parents as some kind of stooge or spy.

"If you don't want to talk about it, we don't have to," I said. "In fact, you don't even have to see me or put up with my sitting here, but I do care about you and your family and if there's anything I can do to help, I want to do it."

I went on talking and shared a little of my own life with her. I shared some of my intimate thoughts and feelings about teenagers I had worked with and the problems I had seen in families. As I talked she stopped crying and began looking right at me. I almost cheered out loud because I knew that eye-to-eye contact with this desperate girl was a special breakthrough. As we talked and I continued to show her I wouldn't condemn her, she began to open up. And of course, when she began sharing what was inside, out came a lot of hostility and anger. As we talked, the hostility and anger seemed to lessen slightly, and I finally asked her if it would be all right to come back and see her the next day.

"That will be okay," she said, and we exchanged waves as I went out the door.

I was back the next day and she looked a little better. She seemed to be in better spirits but still depressed. As we wound up our second conversation, I made a specific point of telling her that she didn't have to talk to me or see me anymore. It was something she'd have to decide. I only wanted to be there if I could really help her.

It was then she asked me the question: "Well, what do you think I ought to do about my problem?"

At that moment I knew I had finally broken all the way through. Now she was asking my opinion. By asking that question, she was saying, "I value your opinion; tell me what you think."

I had finally earned the girl's respect. I had paid my dues and she was now interested in knowing what I thought about what she should do. This is what respect is all about.

It would have been easy to walk in and be very "professional" with the girl. It would have been easy to put her on an even deeper guilt trip than she was already experiencing. Instead, I had to be soft, gentle, and understanding. I had to show her I cared, and I did care!

The ending of the story is a positive one. The young lady got her head straight, overcame some of the overwhelming obstacles she was facing, and made good progress in a relatively short period of time.

In some ways, of course, it might have been easier for me to earn the respect of the desperate teenager in the hospital than it is for a parent to earn the respect of little Festus or Zelda on a 24-hour-a-day, 365-days-a-year basis. But it can and must be done. And one of the telltale signs that you have your child's respect is the question, "Hey, Mom [or Dad], what do you think about this?"

Naturally, you won't always agree with your child on everything. But as long as you have love and respect for each other, the relationship will grow and become stronger and stronger. I often tell parents of younger children that now is the time to build respect between you and your child. It will be like money in the bank when your child hits the teenage years and tensions mount.

From Giving Choices to Pulling Rugs

But what, you may ask, does building respect and giving choices have to do with "pulling the rug"? A great deal, as the following illustration shows.

Choices have to be appropriate, of course. You don't talk with a twelve-year-old about whether or not he wants to drive the family car. You don't tell a six-year-old that he has a choice: he can play with his toy truck or Daddy's shotgun. But many everyday choices are there for the child to make, if we allow him to do so. We can give him the choice of what he wants for lunch that day: "Tommy, would you like a tuna sandwich or peanut butter and jelly?"

We give Tommy the choice, but we teach him that once he makes his decision he does not have the prerogative to change his mind. If we want to use Reality Discipline, we have to show Tommy that if he changes his mind there will be a consequence of some kind. That's how life works. In other words, we must hold him accountable for his choice.

But what happens in many homes? A typical scene is that

after Tommy chooses peanut butter and jelly and Mom has it all prepared, he decides he wants tuna instead. So, Mom wraps up the peanut butter and jelly and tries to save it for another day and dutifully makes Tommy his tuna sandwich.

What is Mom teaching Tommy when she allows him to change his mind at this point? Ironically, she is teaching Tommy to be irresponsible because she is taking an irresponsible position. Here is a beautiful opportunity to let reality come into Tommy's life and teach him a truth that he can use all his days. What I am saying is this: give Tommy the choice between eating his first choice (peanut butter and jelly) or not eating at all. If Tommy chooses not to eat peanut butter and jelly, don't force it down his throat. Put it away and try to keep it fresh for later. But for Tommy, lunch is now over. He is free to play or do whatever he wants to do, but he gets nothing else to eat.

Tommy may shrug and go off to play, but reality may soon move in to teach its lesson. Reality will come in the form of hunger.

Before dinner—quite possibly *well* before dinner—Tommy will be back to the kitchen whining about how hungry he is. This is a crucial moment for at least two reasons: 1) Mom may feel a pang of guilt and sympathy for Tommy. But she must pray for strength and not give in. 2) She must explain to Tommy why he can't have anything to eat until dinner time. She has to tell Tommy clearly and simply that making decisions is important—even simple ones such as what sandwich we plan to eat. She might say something like this: "Yes, I'll bet you are hungry. Since you didn't eat any lunch, you must be starved! Well, you're in luck. We're going to have dinner in about two hours and twenty minutes, right after Daddy gets home. Now run along and play and we'll see you at half-past six."

And so, clutching his hunger-knotted stomach in agony, Tommy goes back out to play. He may shed a tear or two, or at least make some remarks about how mean Mom is. But reality has now moved in to finish "pulling the rug." The rug pulling started back at lunch when Mom put away the peanut butter and jelly sandwich, but refused to make the tuna. Now that Tommy faces a little real hunger for a couple of hours, the rug has been pulled indeed.

And what has Tommy learned? The goal is to teach him that it is a very poor decision not to eat what Mom prepared for lunch. It is a poor decision to change one's mind after it is too late. It is a good decision to go ahead with one's choice even if one believes he might prefer something else at the moment.

Taking the Buzzard by the Beak

Does all this sound too mean and heartless? Some mothers I counsel accuse me of having a cold, "male oriented" attitude.

"It's all right for you, the father, to talk about letting the child go hungry," they say. "You're at work and you don't have to look him in the eye."

I tell these mothers that I understand. At our house, Sande and I try to split up the rug-pulling chores as much as possible. As for being "cold," I smile and say that nothing could be further from the truth. For proof I invite the protesting mother to ask my own kids if I am cold and cruel. Sande and I have been pulling the rug and letting Holly, Krissy, and Kevin tumble all their lives and our little buzzards don't appear to be any worse for the wear. The reason? We love them with all that is in us and they know it!

We don't pull the rug out as a form of punishment or vengeance. We don't pull the rug out to dominate our children or take parental ego trips. We pull the rug with love (and sometimes it takes tremendous commitment to do it because it hurts). It would be easier to just hug them, cuddle them, and coddle them, but this would not teach them the accountability and responsibility they need to face life later. There will be a day when our kids are too big for a lot of hugging and cuddling. And that is when our love will still be touching their lives in a tangible sense as they go about the task of being accountable and responsible adults.

I also like to think that pulling the rug out is a good way to emulate the master role model of Reality Discipline: our Lord Jesus. Yes, He taught us to turn the other cheek, but on many occasions He took the bull by the horns and got things done. He was kind and compassionate, but He was also firm and direct as He pulled the rug on Peter, James, and John, the rich young ruler, and any number of others you might think of.

And that's what Reality Discipline is all about: going into action, taking the bull by the horns (more precisely, taking our little buzzards by the beaks), and pulling the rug with kindness and compassion. There is no better way to demonstrate real love.

I recall one family in which the parents were ruled by Todd, age five. Pulling the rug was a totally repulsive idea for Todd's parents—especially Mom.

Todd was the baby of the family and like many children born last, he was fussy. He liked only certain things, especially when it came to eating. He liked potatoes mashed, but not boiled or baked. He liked his pancakes spread out on the plate, not stacked on top of one another. Todd was indeed a picky child and somewhat of a perfectionist.

Naturally, there were all kinds of hassles at meals. Todd's older brother and sister would usually eat whatever was put before them, but not Todd. He often turned the family dinner hour into a miniwar.

Todd's father did not share his son's perfectionist approach to pancakes or potatoes. He had been raised to not speak unless spoken to and to do what he was told and that was it. Having a child who would rebel over something as simple as eating or not eating his dinner was too much for Dad to take. Down would come his fist on the table and terror reigned supreme around the dinner table. But it seldom got Todd to eat any better.

I tried to help these parents by telling them that they need to give children choices. I explained that the family dinner table is a perfect place to give a child a choice to eat or not to eat. I helped them outline a simple strategy and they went back home to put it into action.

Dinner that evening featured fried chicken. Todd took one look and one sniff and said, "I don't like it! I don't like chicken."

Mom was puzzled because Todd had eaten two helpings of chicken last week, but she didn't go into her usual routine of, "Honey, of course you like chicken. Just last week you had two helpings, and besides, if you eat your chicken you'll get your special strawberry shortcake for dessert."

I had explained to Mom that this kind of talk is useless and even harmful. It doesn't do a thing to get a child to eat.

Instead, Mom quietly picked up Todd's plate, went over to the kitchen sink, and with a flick of the wrist, Todd's dinner was over.

Now, I'm not sure what went through Todd's mind but he might have been thinking, *Mom has finally flipped. She said I was driving her crazy and I think it just happened. She's always telling me how much food costs and she just threw my dinner in the garbage.*

Was Mom's action too severe? Should she have talked it over with Todd and tried to reason with him? She had already tried that many times. No, I believe her action was correct. It is always the perfect disciplinary action with kids who won't eat what is put before them. It actually gives them the right to choose either to eat or not to eat. And it holds them accountable if they choose to be picky or fussy, because the final pull on the rug in this case is that there are no snacks, no treats, nothing at bedtime. They are free to leave the table. They can play, do their homework, whatever their usual routine is, and there will be no punishment. But there is discipline. And the discipline says, "Hey, Mom and Dad aren't going to play the bribery game. We aren't going to have a hassle and shouting and slamming fists on the table. We're just not going to play that kind of game anymore. If you don't want to eat dinner, dinner is over. There will be no cookies, no treats, no anything. It's just good-bye and see you at breakfast."

In Todd's case, his mother recalls that he ate one of the biggest breakfasts of his life. And after that first heroic move on her part (and I use the word *heroic* because I know how hard this was for Mom), she started giving Todd other choices but never the choice to be picky or fussy. And life improved immeasureably in that family.

When parents are brave enough to pull the rug out, they are giving their child the best training possible. They are giving him the opportunity to make a good or poor choice. I believe home should be the place to make good or poor choices. The last place home should be is a place where you are punished for making poor choices. In too many homes I see parents making far too much out of so little. When the milk spills, or the spaghetti is dumped on the dinner table, we don't need sharp words, shouting, a slap, or a thrashing. We need a rag and a kind word that lets the child know that "accidents happen."

Of course, kids don't always think that pulling the rug and using the principle of action and not words is fair. As I said in an earlier chapter, they are masters at trying to put parents on guilt trips. They argue with the skill of accomplished lawyers about what is fair and not fair, when they've been warned and haven't been warned.

But parents have to be firm. They should set up the guidelines and let the child know that if he crosses the line, the rug will be pulled.

For example, parents often complain that their children abuse their toys. I tell them that if little Harold seems to be doing his best to disassemble his video game, simply move in and very calmly take the game away. Yes, little Harold may be upset, but you will accomplish several things. You save the toy and demonstrate to Harold that toys cost money and we don't abuse them. More important, however, you keep order in your home, and you teach Harold to have respect for his possessions as well as yours.

Taking away a toy from a young child who is playing with it in a destructive manner is not punishment. It doesn't say, "I don't love you." It doesn't say, "I don't care about you." What it does say is, "As your parent I can't allow you to misuse this toy. Toys cost money and you can't destroy them just because you think it's fun."

What about a situation where the child actually breaks a toy (or anything else for that matter)? If the child is old enough to get an allowance, an excellent disciplinary measure is to have him pay for a new toy out of his own money. Here is another example of how the allowance can be a tremendous teacher of accountability and responsibility. It's interesting to me that the picture most people get when I talk about pulling the rug out is that the child will land right on his wallet. And, of course, when I talk about pulling the rug, I'm not talking about actually trying to hurt the child in any way. But when you can have the child learn through realizing that poor decisions and poor behavior result in paying through the pocketbook, you are giving him a taste of reality indeed.

Anything Is Easier Than Real Discipline

Basically, I have used this entire chapter to demonstrate one thing: anything is easier than real discipline. It's much easier to be permissive and to just "let it go." And it is even easier to punish because you allow yourself the luxury of letting off steam and you usually don't have to follow through and make sure your child actually learns something. We like to think we'll "teach little Harold a lesson" by spanking him, berating him, and sending him to his room. Unfortunately, all we usually teach Harold is that he had better not get caught the next time, or he will bide his time and wait until he can get back at us in one way or another.

It takes real commitment, perseverance, and courage to

discipline your children. It is never easy but it is always worthwhile. And it pays off. I think of the letter I received from a woman in Chicago. She had a typical problem in her family. Her children wanted too much of her attention. In almost every family there is at least one attention getter—the child who makes a career out of gaining the attention of adults and his peers. Sometimes he does it positively by being well behaved, getting good grades, and so on, but often he does do it negatively, and one of his favorite sports is bugging Mom or Dad.

And that's what this lady faced—being bugged, in this case by both of her kids. Her letter mentioned that she had heard me speak at a seminar in Chicago and she was particularly interested in my comments about the technique of "pulling the rug out."

Her letter went on to say:

> I was talking with my girl friend on the telephone and the children were being really obnoxious. I asked them to be quiet at least twice. The third time I remembered what you had said and decided to take action rather than just use words. I put down the phone and escorted the children outside the house. Then I went back to my telephone conversation and talked for at least another twenty minutes.

> As I turned from the phone and looked toward the kitchen window, I saw a little hand with a note in it. The note said, "Mommy, we love you—over." Then they flipped the note over and it said, "We are sorry. Can we come in now?"

I remember actually chuckling with pleasure as I read the mother's letter to me as well as the children's note which she had included. I sent back my own note, thanking her for sharing her experience with me. I told her she was a brave parent to take that kind of action with her children. And I particularly noted one line in her letter which had said that now when she's on the telephone, her children's behavior is

180 degrees in the other direction. Why the change? Because she took action. She took the little buzzards by the beaks. She told them they could continue to be obnoxious if they wanted to, but if that was their choice they would have to do it outside—especially when Mom was on the telephone.

The moral in this mother's story is crystal clear. Our kids really do notice and pay attention when we take firm action and put reality to work. Yes, it would have been easy for that young mother to give in to her children's pleas as she was trying to put them outside. They probably wailed, "Oh, Mommy! We'll be good. Please don't put us outside. We'll be good."

If that mother had bent at that particular moment, she would have lost the whole battle. But she hung in there and followed through. You can do the same; I pray that you are.

Never be afraid to pull the rug out and let the little buzzards tumble. I promise you they will land right side up—and so will you!

5

Danger—Super Parent at Work!

"How can I get my child to like himself better? He seems so unhappy. . . ."

"How can I get my child to achieve his potential? I know he can do better. . . ."

"How do I get my child to be responsible?"

"I'm worried. I see my kid going in the wrong direction—he's only in the fourth grade and he's already running with the wrong crowd."

"What do we do with Billy? He's already rebelling and we've tried so hard to train him up right, the way God wants."

All of the above comments are typical of what I hear from parents almost every week. These comments reflect parental concern for their children, and I sympathize with every one of them. As a parent, I, too, have concerns about my own children. I, too, am bombarded with advice and admonitions on how to do a better job of parenting. There are literally tons of books, articles, pamphlets, tapes, films, and video cassettes out there telling us why and how we should be Super Parent. And I suppose that at several points in this book, I sound just like the rest of the experts:

"Be sure you don't do this. . . . Be sure you do that."

"Be faster than a speeding bullet as you use actions, not words."

"Be more powerful than a locomotive as you enforce the rules of Reality Discipline."

"Leap tall problems with a single bound, to be loving, caring, and aware of your child's feelings."

I understand when a parent gets frustrated with "advice from the experts." I have felt the same kind of frustrations myself—and I'm supposed to be one of the experts! Parenting *is* a difficult task. My first book on parenting was titled *Parenthood Without Hassles—Well, Almost.* While I was confident that parenting could be a much simpler task than a lot of people were making it, I was still aware that *all* the hassles would not disappear.

Now, four years later, I am even a bit more realistic. *Making Children Mind Without Losing Yours* is the name of the Reality Discipline game. And quite possibly, by now, you understand that there is one thing wrong with that title: you don't *make* your child mind. By using the concepts of Reality Discipline, you guide your child toward making wise decisions about the realities of life. And you know he or she won't make all the right decisions. You know you need to give him freedom to fail. Nevertheless, you are positive that he will make more wise decisions than poor ones as he learns to be accountable and responsible by disciplining himself.

What makes what I am saying different from the other "experts"? In some ways, I'm not that different at all. A lot of psychologists and child-rearing specialists believe in discipline, accountability, responsibility, and helping children make wise decisions. But I am still convinced that Reality Discipline has distinctives that need to be practiced in every home where children live.

1. *Parents never seek to punish; they always seek to discipline, train, and teach.*

2. *If "punishment," pain, or some kind of consequence is in-*

volved, the parent is not doing it or causing it—reality is. Your child is learning how the real world works.

3. *Reality Discipline is the best system I know to avoid inconsistent meandering between authoritarianism and permissiveness.* Most parents know instinctively that they should be *authoritative*—in charge but reasonable and fair. Staying with the authoritative happy medium is best done through Reality Discipline.

4. *Reality Discipline is the best system for teaching accountability and responsibility in a way that will stick.* The child learns through making his own decisions and experiencing his own mistakes and failures, as well as his own successes. He is not a puppet or imitator of his parents; he is their student and in the Christian home he is seeking to follow Christ.

5. *Above all, Reality Discipline is your best bet for avoiding what I call the Super Parent Syndrome.* When it comes to parenting, most of us not only want to get off the runway but we also want to make our efforts fly—like a bird, like a plane, even like a space capsule. We want our parenting to *work.* We want to be effective. That's why I like to caution parents, "Be a bird, be a plane, but *not* Super Parent!" In fact, if you are using Reality Discipline concepts at all, they will automatically keep you from making the four key mistakes of a Super Parent. The "Big Four" occur in all kinds of homes, but I have found that Christian families are particularly susceptible. Super Moms and Super Dads often get trapped into the following four kinds of faulty reasoning:

1. I own my children.
2. I am judge and jury.
3. My children can't fail.
4. I am boss—what I say goes.

All four of these erroneous ideas smack of authoritarianism—the style of parenting that is long on control but short on love and support. The authoritarian parent is "in charge," and running things with an infallible and firm hand. It's easy to slip into this kind of thinking when you believe you are doing God's will as you train up your child in the way God wants him to go. Some parents are more authoritarian than others, of course, but it's a role we slip into far too easily, especially if things get out of hand and we get impatient, frustrated, or confused. That's why I believe it's good for parents to be aware of the four pitfalls of the Super Parent Syndrome.

I Own My Children

I believe all parents need to be reminded that they don't own their children. It's true that parenting is a long-term (not to mention expensive) investment. But our children don't belong to us. Reality Discipline reminds us that we aren't trying to own or keep our children; we are trying to help them learn to be responsible and accountable persons in their own right.

Our children belong to the Lord Himself. He has given them to us "on loan," with specific guidelines in His Word for the training and enrichment of their lives. When we slip into the Super Parent Syndrome, we can try so hard and get so wrapped up in our children that we try to possess them. And often we can be quite loving while we do it. I mention above that the authoritarian parent is strong on control and short on love and support. That doesn't mean that there aren't many authoritarian homes where there seems to be a lot of love, but it is a benevolent dictatorship. Reality Discipline is designed to help you strike a balance that shows your child warmth and love but also gives him freedom to make his own decisions. Reality Discipline seeks to guide, not own or control.

I Am Judge and Jury

By the same token, if we are not owners of our children, we are certainly not the judge and jury. The only Judge is God Himself, and all of us will be judged someday. Yes, we have authority over our children but we always use that authority with tender, loving fairness. Challenges arise every day in our lives and the lives of our children. But Reality Discipline stresses that we are not to pass down judgments on our children, even though they often try to involve us in doing just that. Children have a natural tendency to see Mom and Dad as infallible and the final court of appeal to help them get what they want at the time. It is often tempting to step in and solve their problems and pronounce the just decree.

For example, let us look in on Ricky and Bobby, ages six and eight. They have been scrapping and fighting after going to bed. Dad has already come in three times and told them to settle down. But Ricky and Bobby keep wrestling, arguing, and carrying on. Finally, Ricky (the six-year-old) starts to cry. That does it—the anger button is pressed inside Dad and off he goes into their room, determined to settle this—now!

"All right! Who started it?" Dad is now judge and jury, and he's going to find out just where he should dispense proper punishment.

For some strange reason, Ricky and Bobby simply point at each other. Dad's judge-and-jury role becomes confusing, so he says, "Now listen up! I've had it. I've told you guys three times now to settle down and I mean it! DO YOU UNDERSTAND ME?"

"Yes, Daddy."

"Yes, Daddy."

Dad leaves in anger, slamming the bedroom door so hard it shakes the whole house. And what are Ricky and Bobby doing behind the closed bedroom door? They are looking at each other, hands over mouths, trying to stifle their giggles.

Bobby snickers, "Did you see the veins on his neck? I've never seen him get that mad before."

Meanwhile, Dad returns to the living room to try to continue watching television with Mom. Mom adds to the problem by turning to him to say, "John, it seems to me you were entirely too hard on the boys."

John retorts, "Seems to me if you disciplined around here, I wouldn't have to do that!"

Then Super Mom and Super Dad may go back to watching "Hart to Hart" in stony silence, or they may get into a hassle of their own. They have fallen nicely for the strategy of Ricky and Bobby, who have needlessly involved them both in their own little hassle. Ironically enough, while believing he was playing the role of judge and jury, Dad was really being manipulated by his own kids! His first mistake was correcting them three times before they really pressed his button and caused him to commit his second mistake, getting absolutely enraged. His third mistake was asking them, "Who did it?" Of course, neither boy would admit to being guilty.

What should Dad have done? He had several options that could have come out of principles from Reality Discipline. He could have worked out a "logical consequence" that would have told the boys if they continued the hassle, they would wind up having to go to bed earlier on the next several nights. Or, he could have removed one child from the bedroom and made him sleep somewhere else for the night. (For more on how to handle this problem, see "Bedtime Battles" in chapter 7.)

Whatever a parent does, he should never play judge and jury. Parents are not running a court. They are operating a home where encouragement takes the place of reward and discipline always triumphs over punishment. It takes a Super Parent to play the judge-and-jury game. You need the speed of a bullet and the strength of a locomotive. To play the Reality Discipline game, however, you need the wisdom to guide your children in making right decisions and letting reality call the shots.

My Children Can't Fail

When you slip into Super Parent thinking, failure is not a favorable idea. The Super Parent believes he must not and cannot fail because God is on his side. Naturally enough, he believes his children cannot fail either, and if they do fail, he finds this very hard to accept. The feelings of disappointment are interpreted by children as conditional acceptance, and the tension continues to build. The truth is that our children *can* fail.

I believe children should fail on occasion because failure is good for them. Those are bitter words for Super Parents to accept. Several years ago, I was on a radio talk show with Abigail Van Buren of "Dear Abby" fame. Abby had picked up "A Child's Ten Commandments to Parents" from my book *Parenthood Without Hassles—Well, Almost* and had printed them in her column. She stated during the talk show that after printing the column she had gotten more than seven hundred letters from people who didn't like one of the commandments, which read: "Please give me the freedom to make decisions concerning myself. Permit me to fail, so that I can learn from my mistakes. Then someday I'll be prepared to make the kind of decisions life requires of me."

Abby's comment was graphic proof of what the problem is in many homes today. Parents are afraid to let their kids fail. I'm not saying that a child should be a failure by habit or that he should learn to be a loser in life. I am saying that we learn through failure. We learn through making our own decisions, and some of those decisions turn out to be mistakes which lead to failure.

No matter how many letters come in criticizing that "seventh commandment," I still believe the Christian home should be a place where failure is allowed. It is dealt with matter-of-factly and is cushioned with love and encouragement from the parents.

I think of Harlan's father, who had been a super athlete in high school and college. Little Harlan tried out for the major division of his Little League team and didn't make it. He was assigned to a minor league team instead. Without Harlan's knowledge or permission, his dad went to the coach and tried to talk about it. In the process, his dad lost his temper and there was a loud shouting match. Some of the parents and most of the team members, all schoolmates of Harlan, heard the whole thing. Harlan was there, too, and was so embarrassed, he didn't want to show his face around school for months. He wound up quitting his minor league team and would have nothing to do with baseball after that.

Failure *is* difficult for parents to deal with. We want our children to succeed in life and be happy, but we need to ask ourselves some questions: When and how did *we* succeed? Didn't we often succeed out of failure? Didn't we come from failure to victory in many phases of our lives?

I think it's interesting that everyone's Christian life begins with failure. When we come to the saving grace of Christ, we do not come out of victory but out of admitting defeat. We are sinners and we need a Savior. As we admit our mistakes and our need of Christ, it is then that we have victory.

I Am Boss—What I Say Goes

The parent who uses Reality Discipline is in authority but never the boss. In the Christian home, God is boss. The parent is only managing what God has provided. With Reality Discipline, you seek to help your child become accountable and responsible, but you do not make his or her decisions. When you slip into the Super Parent type of thinking, you start making decisions for your children because "you know best."

True, every parent knows more than his children (most of the time!). There are many situations where a parent knows what a child should do because the parent has been down that road before.

But Reality Discipline helps you guide the child, not dominate him and make his decisions for him. It is more trouble to guide a child, but it is infinitely more worthwhile. A parent can make all of his child's decisions, but what happens when the child reaches junior high, high school, college, and adulthood? I often deal with counseling situations that are tragic and at their base is a parent who is still trying to make decisions for his grown, or practically grown, child.

Not long ago, I worked with a fifteen-year-old girl I'll call Sarah. She was a teenager whose mom and dad knew exactly what was best for her. The parents totally bottled up Sarah. She had no freedom; she was watched, suspected, not trusted. There was never any evidence that Sarah was rebellious or was doing anything wrong. The parents had no reason not to trust her, but they didn't anyway.

Sarah could go to church, but when there was any kind of outing by the youth groups such as miniature golf, skating, and so on, the parents said a flat no. Sarah never had any dates, not even with a group of her peers.

At age fifteen, she turned up in my office—pregnant. She had been climbing out of her window at night to meet a nineteen-year-old boy. The parents had good intentions, but their ignorance of the freedom that children need to learn and to grow caused terrible tragedy. The parents were beside themselves when they finally realized that they had contributed to their daughter's downfall. The girl had always viewed her parents as insensitive and strict. She saw what they did to her as punishment and she said to herself, *Okay, Mom and Dad, if you have the right to punish me, I have the right to punish you.* And she got back at them, only to leave her life in ruins.

I often see parents trying to decide for their children where they will go to school—what college they will attend. Then they decide what job or profession the child should have. Many parents are even involved in deciding whom the child should marry. I'm not saying that parents shouldn't have input about schooling, professions, and marriage partners, but input and opinions are far different from control and pressure which parents can often apply.

Then there is that greatest decision of all. Can any parent make his child's decision to accept Christ as Savior? Not even a Super Parent can pull that one off!

The above are just a few examples of how Super Parent thinking leads you down the wrong road every time. Trying to be Super Parent can only cause problems, and if you are a normal family, you already have enough problems to work on. Of course, if you are desperately trying to be Super Parent, you don't like admitting that the problems are there. But there is nothing wrong with having problems. We all have them. The question is, how do we respond to them?

Is Your Family Healthy or Unhealthy?

All families are worried about good health. It's not uncommon for parents to spend thousands of dollars on being sure their families eat properly, get decent medical care, and so on. You can do all that, and still have an unhealthy home. The unhealthy part comes from how you, the parents, are responding to the problems that are a part of everyday living. Without trying to push the health analogy too far, I think we can look at problems as we look at germs. Do we let problems infect our families and turn into serious disease? Or can we absorb the problems, fight off the ill effects, and stay healthy?

An instance of unhealthy behavior that I see in quite a few families is their treatment of the "black sheep." Parents will call and make an appointment for family therapy. Then they will bring in little Buford or Cletus and essentially say to me, "Doc, this is the one. This is the one who walks to a different beat. This is the one who rebels against church. This is the one who gets the poor grades. Fix him!"

And the black sheep usually sits there and hangs his head or stares out the window, looking bored to death. My reaction usually surprises the parents. I tell them that if we're going to make any headway in changing Buford's behavior, then we must all consider changing our own behavior first.

Whenever I deal with a family who believes it has a "black sheep" child, I frequently ask the entire family to meet with me. It's important that the family see the misbehavior of one child not as just that child's problem. It is the entire family's problem. Usually there are reasons for the child's behavior and often the family members are contributing to what is going on.

For example, it's not difficult to miss seeing the payoff a model child gets from having a black-sheep brother or sister a year and a half or so behind him. (Or, perhaps the black sheep is the older child.) Every time the model child does something right, it only makes the black sheep look worse. In many families, the more a model child behaves well, the more he helps destroy the self-esteem and confidence of his black-sheep sibling. The model child would never admit it verbally, but he is definitely getting a payoff out of all this. His own position in the family is enhanced by his black-sheep brother's or sister's misbehavior. Parents are only human. They do compare and they wonder why little Buford can't be like his model older sister.

The question then arises, "All right, what do we do with Buford? Is his model brother or sister supposed to start acting like a black sheep, too, so everyone feels comfortable?"

Of course not, but what families, and especially parents, need to do is look for the purpose behind Buford's temper tantrums, thumb sucking, antisocial behavior, and so on. I try to help parents identify behavior—positive and negative—and then deal with it differently than they have been. The responses by parents and other family members can do much to reinforce unwanted behavior in a child; likewise, family responses can reinforce desirable behavior. It depends on the response, which can be healthy or unhealthy. The chart on pages 98 and 99 illustrates what I mean. It gives

BEHAVIOR	UNHEALTHY PARENTAL RESPONSE	CHILD'S PERCEPTION OF SELF	HEALTHY PARENTAL RESPONSE	CHILD'S PERCEPTION OF SELF
Child "forgets" to do his chores and goes off to play with his friends. (Negative)	"You are so irresponsible!" "You will never amount to anything if you don't learn to get your work done." "You're grounded for a week."	"I am bad. I'm not worth much." "I'm being punished and it's not fair."	"I really get upset when the chores aren't done. I had to hire the neighbor's boy to do your work. It cost five dollars, and it will be deducted from your allowance." "You won't be going to the scout meeting tonight because you have to stay home and do the chores you didn't do this afternoon."	"Mom is angry because I didn't do my chores." "If I don't do them, I will have to pay the price. She's giving me the choice."
Child helps Mom wash the dishes and clean up the kitchen. (Positive)	"Here's a dollar for helping Mom." "My, you are such a good boy for helping Mommy."	"Mom likes me as long as I'm good." "I can get money for helping her."	"Thanks for your hard work. I appreciate it." "Having help has made this job a lot easier." "Thank you. The kitchen looks great, doesn't it?"	"I am important. I belong to this family." "I am responsible and I do a good job."

Child is caught cutting classes at school. (Negative)	"How could you do this to us?" "You're a sneak and a liar!" "You'll wind up in reform school."	"I'm no good." "All my parents worry about is how they look to the teachers at school." "I'm going to wind up a punk so I might as well be one."	"I'm sorry to hear that you seem to dislike school that much." "Let's talk about it and try to find out what's bugging you." "I could be wrong, but I think you need school, for a lot of reasons."	"My parents are concerned about me." "They want to hear my side."
Child cleans room by herself. (Positive)	"It looks all right but you forgot to hang up your sweater." "You're such a dear for helping Mommy by cleaning your room." "You made God very happy."	"I never do anything right." "Mommy loves me because I cleaned my room." "God only loves me when I do as I'm told."	"Your room looks great." "I'll bet you're proud of your work. Nice job!" "Your effort paid off. What a terrific-looking room!"	"I'm responsible—I can work without Mom being there." "I can discipline myself. I can do it."

examples of some positive and negative behaviors, healthy and unhealthy parental responses, and the child's perception of himself after each kind of response.

The unhealthy parental responses in the two negative examples of behavior are easy to spot. In both cases, the parent sends a "you" message that is loud and clear. It says to the child, in so many words, "You are no good, not worth much, disappointing, and headed for more trouble."

Many children hear this kind of message all the time and instead of improving, they get worse. Parents reinforce the child's negative behavior by telling him he's no good and won't be able to improve. So, the child fulfills the prophecy.

Healthier responses to a child when he does something negative are in the form of the "I" message, which lets the child know the parent is hurt, angry, and concerned. But instead of attacking the child, the parent simply shares feelings and concerns and asks the child to work with him to improve the situation.

Now let's take a look at the two samples of positive behavior and the unhealthy and healthy responses. The unhealthy responses are very common ones. They may be similar to responses we have gotten from our own parents. For example, "You are such a good boy for helping Mommy."

Now, what's wrong with that? What's wrong with telling the child he's a good boy?

There is quite a bit that is wrong, but it is difficult to spot. The remark conveys that the child is loved *because* he helped Mommy. It implies that he is loved only when he helps. What might be going on in the child's mind when he hears this kind of response? He might be thinking, *What if I didn't help? Wouldn't I be loved?*

While the child may not be able to verbalize it, he might be thinking that the parent's love is conditional. If he doesn't perform, he doesn't get loved. What a parent should always try to convey to any child is that the child is loved whether he helps or not, whether he performs well or not.

Now let's look at the healthy responses: "Having help sure

made this job a lot easier"; "Thank you"; and "The kitchen looks great, doesn't it?"

These statements send the child positive messages. The child hears that his work is appreciated. The emphasis is on the job and not on the child. He learns that he made the job easier for his mother and his mother is thankful. This makes him feel good and worthwhile. And then to hear that the "kitchen looks great" lets him know he is capable—that he can do a good job.

The examples on the chart on pages 98 and 99 give you the basic concept of the difference between healthy and unhealthy parental responses to typical problems in the home. Study the chart and think about how healthy your responses to your children usually are. Are you using encouragement and loving discipline, or are you slipping into the unhealthy modes of praise and punishment?

I urge all Christian parents to commit Ephesians 6:4 to memory as a means of continually reminding themselves of the difference between healthy and unhealthy responses to their children. *The Living Bible* says it so well: "Don't keep on scolding and nagging your children, making them angry and resentful. Rather, bring them up with the loving discipline the Lord himself approves, with suggestions and godly advice."

In this single verse, the Apostle Paul has painted a perfect portrait of Reality Discipline. The parent described in Ephesians 6:4 avoids frustrating and dominating his child while attempting to nurture him as God intends. Unfortunately, I see too many Christian moms and dads trying to be Super Parents because they sincerely think this is what Scripture teaches. Ironically enough, these Christian Super Parents depend more on themselves than on God. They may talk about trusting God, but their parenting style reveals that their basic trust is in themselves. They seem to enjoy the role of judge and jury or answer man or lady. They push so hard for excellence that their children are frozen by fear of failure.

And sometimes a Super Parent's striving for excellence can result in wearing that parent out completely, while he or she acts as slave or servant to the family. This often happens to mothers. For example, I once counseled Michelle, a perfectionist thirty-four-year-old mother who had three daughters, the oldest in junior high school. Michelle's girls were easy to spot. Their color-coordinated outfits could be seen from more than a block away. Michelle even ironed the bacon for breakfast to be sure it was flat and "neat looking."

When Michelle came to me, she was a thoroughly exhausted woman—physically and emotionally. She was up every morning at 5:30 A.M. She had a battle every day getting the girls out of bed, making sure their teeth were brushed, and so on. At 6:45 A.M., perfectly dressed and groomed, she would serve her family four different breakfasts. One daughter would have blueberry pancakes, another scrambled eggs, and the third cereal. Dad, of course, would usually have his favorite, eggs Benedict.

This idiocy went on day in and day out and finally Michelle started to crack. Her family was a circus and she was trying to be ringmaster. She was an extreme and pathetic illustration of the kind of mother who wants to give her family everything. What she was doing was contrary to sound psychology, good common sense, and biblical wisdom. After several weeks of therapy, Michelle finally made some progress. Her most significant act was to finally throw up her hands and announce that she was "going on strike." She did just that, stopped trying to be "Super Mom," and the entire situation improved rapidly.

Ironically, while Michelle believed that she was giving her family love, and while she was certainly trying to act lovingly, she was not achieving her goals at all. By making so many decisions for her children and by constantly "doing for them," she actually hampered their development into responsible persons who could make their own decisions and learn accountability to others, and ultimately to God.

The Ultimate Goal of Reality Discipline

The most important questions parents ask me at the seminars I conduct throughout the United States and Canada are, "How do I help my child develop spiritually? How do I enhance my child's relationship with God?"

I think the key to answering these questions centers around the Reality Discipline concept of action, not words. Children hear many words about God in their home. They hear many words in Sunday school and church. But they don't always see much action that seems connected to facing God. As they grow older, they often have difficulties with the weakness and hypocrisy of the adults around them. They see the humanness in their parents and others in their homes and churches.

There is nothing wrong with being human, but there is a great deal wrong with being hypocritical. I believe that when I freely admit my humanness to my children, I am taking advantage of an ideal opportunity to teach them dependence upon the grace of God. As I admit to my children that I don't always have all the answers and as I pray with them and share with them, they see me depending upon the strength of the Holy Spirit and my walk with Jesus Christ as I deal with the everyday hassles of life.

One of the best ways to show (not just tell) your children you are truly dependent upon God is through prayer. Do you take time to pray regularly with your children? I'm not talking about sitting on your child's bed just before he goes to sleep and reciting, "Now I lay me down to sleep, I pray this Lord, my soul to keep, like little birdies in their nests, angels guide me while I rest. . . ." My children have never heard that kind of prayer. When I pray with them, I want to pray about the day, about our needs, about specific problems, whatever they might be. I pray with our children for Grandma or Grandpa, for Mom and Dad, or for brother or sister. I pray with them about something we are particularly thankful for that day—a need that was met or an answer that came.

I also pray with our children about my weaknesses and shortcomings. My children do not hear me thanking God for my perfection. They hear me depending on Him for wisdom and strength.

Children look up to adults. Adults are so much bigger and they can do so much more. Adults meet the needs of children throughout the day. It's no wonder that little children actually see their fathers and mothers as "perfect."

Of course, the mantle of perfection soon drops in tatters from our shoulders. But as long as we have them fooled, we are not doing them any favors with our masquerade. One problem is that when someone sees anyone else as perfect, he tends to be uncomfortable. Perfect people are not easy to be around. They don't seem that approachable, and if there's anything I want to be as a parent to my children, it is approachable.

It is sad to see so many parents—out of pride or selfishness—refuse to let their children know that they do have flaws and that they don't have it all together. When parents are brave enough to share their flaws and lacks with their children through prayer, they serve as beautiful models of what it means to depend on God. When you are open and transparent before God and your children, you are saying that, "even though I am many years older, I, too, depend on our heavenly Father, just as I want you to depend on Him."

Another benefit of being open before God and your children is that it will motivate them to seek you out and talk about their real feelings. They are more likely to share their problems and weaknesses with you, if they know that you have been down that same road yourself. They will reason, *Mommy won't be mad about this because she had it happen, too.*

I think prayer time is the most special time of the day for you and your children. I urge you parents to hold your children as you pray. Take your time and don't hurry. Really speak from the heart. Stay away from cute prayers and prayers that you can memorize. Teach your children to pray from the heart and teach them to pray for their every need.

Show your child that you are depending on the all-encompassing love and strength of Christ in your life. Model submission to the Lord before your child and he will learn how to submit his own life to God.

Make prayer a priority in your home, along with going to church and Sunday school. Take time to have devotions around the dinner table. Take every opportunity to have the courage to share your innermost thoughts and feelings about your heavenly Father. Your children will learn to do the same.

I believe that modeling submission to God results in a double blessing: 1) you take definite steps toward your ultimate goal—to guide your child to make his own decisions, especially the decision to accept Christ as Lord of his life; 2) you fulfill your role of the authoritative parent, which Paul describes in Ephesians 6:4. Note, I said *authoritative,* not *authoritarian.* The authoritative parent stands on the solid middle ground between the extremes of permissiveness and authoritarianism. As the chart on page 107 describes, neither the permissive or the authoritarian parent helps the child learn to make decisions. The permissive parent robs the child of self-respect and a sense of initiative by doing so much *for* him. The authoritarian parent robs the child of self-esteem and a sense of independence by doing so much *to* him.

The authoritarian parent controls the child with autocratic rule, but such despotism is doomed to ineffectiveness. The autocratic authoritarian may think his child is "toeing the mark," but in actuality this parent has made himself accountable for the child's behavior. Authoritarianism invites rebellion because it fosters two kinds of behavior in the child. One kind is for the parents and other authority figures to see. The other kind is what the child does when on his own or out with his friends. Believe me, these behaviors can be radically different.

One of the laments I hear almost every week is, "Little Festus is one way at home, but when he's with his friends, he's always in trouble."

When I can identify a parent's style as autocratic and authoritarian, I gently ask, "What can you expect? You have deprived your child of the opportunity to make decisions about life. You have been emphasizing control but neglecting to teach him to be independent and self-confident in his own decisions."

I believe the Christian home should be a place where children can learn to make decisions about their lives and learn to accept the consequences of their decisions—the good and the bad. The home is really a tuition-free university where children study the lifelong curriculum of decision making. I say free because God has given us free will. We can make our own decisions, including whether or not to accept or reject His offer of eternal love and salvation. The freedom we have is one of the great proofs of how much God loves us.

The home ought to be a reflection of that kind of love. God is in authority over the parents but gives them freedom and love. The parents are in authority over the children, and the children should also have freedom and love.

This sounds dangerous to some parents. They keep grasping the concept of control. If they do not control their child, he will get out of hand, he will get hurt, he will go the wrong way, and so on. But if you stop to think, the parent has no other real choice than to give his child freedom. I'm not saying he should neglect his child or let him run into the street and get killed. But at the base of the child-parent relationship should be the parent's desire to train the child, guide him, and set him free to become his own person. The child is becoming an individual anyway, and instead of cramping and crimping the process, you should encourage it and enhance it.

THE AUTHORI-TARIAN PARENT	THE AUTHORITA-TIVE OR RESPON-SIBLE PARENT	THE PERMISSIVE PARENT
1. Makes all decisions for the child.	1. Gives the child choices and formulates guidelines with him or her.	1. Is a slave to the child.
2. Uses reward and punishment to *control* child's behavior.	2. Provides the child with decision-making opportunities.	2. Places priority on the child, not on his or her spouse.
3. Sees himself as *better than* the child.	3. Develops consistent, loving discipline.	3. Robs the child of self-respect and self-esteem by doing things for him that the child can do for himself.
4. Runs the home with an iron hand; grants little freedom to the child.	4. Holds the child accountable.	4. Provides the child with the "Disneyland" experience; makes things as easy as possible— does homework for the child, answers for the child, and so on.
	5. Lets reality be the teacher.	5. Invites rebellion with inconsistent parenting.
	6. Conveys respect, self-worth, and love to the child and therefore enhances the child's self-esteem.	

Your child will soon be an adolescent and then an adult. He will soon do what he wants anyway (and this comes much sooner than you think). Even as early as the teenage years, we basically don't have a lot to go on but our child's love and respect. We may think we have power and control, but it is fast slipping away.

I deal with parents all the time who have not granted freedom to their children, and they are now reaping bitter fruit as the children become teenagers and young adults. The entire thrust of this book is to help you train up your child from his earliest years to make wise decisions. You can have no greater goal as a parent.

6

The Way to Be Your Child's Best Friend

So far, we have looked at some basic principles behind Reality Discipline. These concepts include the following:

Reality Disciplinarians try to be consistent, decisive, and respectful of their children as persons.

Reality Disciplinarians use guidance rather than force, but they are action-oriented, not satisfied to just use words.

Reality Disciplinarians hold their children accountable for their actions, whatever those actions are, to help their children learn from experience. That experience may include failure or success, but in all cases the children are responsible and accountable for what they do.

Reality Disciplinarians are concerned about helping their children learn. They realize they are the most important teachers their children can ever have, but they also seek the best possible school situations for their children.

Perhaps you cringe a bit when I use the term *Reality Disciplinarian.* Our normal concept of a disciplinarian is someone who is strict, authoritarian, and generally not too much fun to live with. What I'm hoping to do in this book, however, is to show you that by being a disciplinarian, you will be the best friend your child ever had. A disciplinarian is someone who guides, trains, and teaches to help another person become more mature, responsible, and succcessful in life.

Reject the Behavior, Love the Child

And the bottom line is that children want discipline. They will not reject you because you are a disciplinarian as long as they are sure you are not rejecting them. And that is the beauty of the Reality Discipline concept. Reality Discipline allows parents to communicate to their children that they love them even though they don't always love their behavior. It is quite possibly the key problem in homes today. My practice in counseling, along with the seminars I conduct all over the country, shows me again and again that parents are unskilled in the art of helping their children see that, "I love you but I don't like what you did." Somehow the children continue to get the message that, "you don't like what I did and you don't like me very much either."

But the children keep coming back for more. They keep testing and rebelling and probing and all the time they are asking one basic question: "Do you love me? Do you love me enough to discipline me and correct me, but at the same time, do you still like me?"

Balance is a key word when using Reality Discipline. The child misbehaves and you must deal with it. If you deal with it in too permissive a manner, the child will soon decide that he is running the house. If you deal with it with too much of the authoritarian approach, the child will feel that you are trampling him and bide his time until he can get back at you in one way or another. "Getting back" can run the gamut from being sassy or disobedient, all the way to running away or suicide. The tragedy that I see repeatedly happening is rebellious children who literally destroy their lives as they seek to retaliate against parental authoritarianism.

Some children reared in authoritarian homes remain "good little boys and girls" until they reach upper adolescence or early adulthood, and then they get their revenge through open rebellion, rejection of their faith, and so on. And I have counseled many adults who don't rebel until later in life. Many a "midlife crisis" is a man or a woman working out feelings about an authoritarian upbringing.

Always Keep Short Accounts

Reality Discipline seeks to not be too permissive and not be too authoritarian. You try to be consistent and always action-oriented. A parent using Reality Discipline keeps short accounts. There isn't a lot of saving up of resentment or anger or frustration. When a rule is broken or another kind of misbehavior occurs, the child knows that there will be an immediate settlement of the situation.

And, as I have pointed out, a "settlement" does not necessarily mean an immediate swat or spanking. There is a place for corporal punishment but I believe too many parents use it when they don't have to. The key issue in any situation that calls for discipline is that the child sees what he did wrong, that he has an opportunity to repent and feel sorry, and that he feels that he's been dealt with fairly.

In some cases a child may feel truly sorry and express his repentance to the offended person. If the child has asked for forgiveness, he should be forgiven. What is important is to communicate. If possible, the child and his mother or father should talk about the situation. It is during this time of talking about a misbehavior or a breaking of rules that real training takes place. With Reality Discipline you are not disciplining your child simply for the sake of disciplining him or even for the sake of "keeping order." Your long-range goal is to help your child become an accountable and responsible person who learns how to discipline himself.

Use Your Most Powerful Ally

As you train your child with Reality Discipline, always make good use of your most powerful ally: natural or logical consequences. The concept of "natural consequences" was first developed by psychiatrist Rudolf Dreikurs. Dreikurs believed that the best way to train children is to let life do the work. Many consequences are "natural" in that they will simply happen if events are left to take their course. The Scripture nicely describes natural consequences in Galatians 6:7. To paraphrase the verse slightly, "A child reaps what he sows." For example:

Run when you should walk and you slip and scrape your knee.

Eat too much candy and get cavities.

Stay up too late and be late for school the next day.

"Logical" consequences are a little different. The parents set logical consequences up ahead of time by talking to the child about what will happen if certain responsibilities are not met. For example:

Refuse to eat your dinner, and it goes in the garbage (or to Bowser) and you get nothing to eat until breakfast.

Come home late from your friend's house and you can't go there tomorrow (or you have to come home sooner the next time).

Repeatedly forget to feed the cat and we have to find a new home for the cat.

As you use natural or logical consequences with your child, be willing to explain things but don't go over and over the ground rules and don't give a lot of warnings, extra chances, and so on. One of your key goals is to teach your child that consequences in life are very real and life doesn't always give a second chance.

Daily living gives you constant opportunities to put natural or logical consequences into action. And every time you do, be ready for that critical "moment of truth" when the consequence has to occur. If you weaken or become too permissive, your discipline not only lacks reality; it will lack results as well.

Remorse Can Be a Child's Weapon

As a parent, I realize it isn't always easy to hang tough and enforce logical or natural consequences. It can be downright painful to let natural consequences take their course as you let little Buford sleep in and he is late for school. There will be wails, tears, and remorse, all of which can be nerve-racking.

I often caution parents to be aware that their child's remorse can be very real, but possibly is a manipulative weapon. If your child is continually breaking the same rule or doing the same thing wrong and continuing to show remorse, he may be using it as a weapon. He may be learning that, *as long as I tell Mommy I'm sorry, I can get away with it.* Keep in mind that Reality Discipline always asks for accountability. Remorse is good, but in many cases it is not enough. For example, when a child breaks something in a home through violating a direct rule such as "no roughhousing," he may show a great deal of remorse. But he's also to be held accountable for what he broke.

The same principle of accountability would hold true for a child who is continually late for dinner. You might accept his apology on one or two occasions, but if the behavior continues, the child will have to wind up not having any dinner.

I remember a nine-year-old young lady I was working with in a number of counseling sessions. She was eagerly looking forward to spending a certain weekend with her girl friend. She was going to stay overnight at the girl friend's house, have breakfast the next morning, and then they were going on a special outing with her friend's mother.

But our nine-year-old young miss also had a number of chores that had to be done each week by Friday evening. All the chores were predetermined and the time limits were clearly set by Mom.

Friday rolled around and at 6:30 P.M. the daughter reminded Mom that now was the time to go to her girl friend's house. The only problem was that her chores were not finished. In fact, most of them weren't even started. Mom calmly said, "Honey, I'm sorry, but you're not going to be able to go."

Naturally there were tears and a scene, but after things calmed down, the daughter returned to the table, still teary-eyed, and said, "But Mommy ... why?"

Mother calmly said, "Honey, because the chores that you were to do after school today weren't done. I'm sorry, but you're going to have to stay home this evening and finish those chores."

What happened next is interesting and most significant to parents who are interested in using Reality Discipline. With all the skill and wisdom that children seem to possess, the nine-year-old daughter started chastising her mother.

"But Mom ... you didn't tell me I had to do this! How come you didn't warn me?"

See how easy it is to create a monster—if you please, a "little buzzard"? Our children are so very adept at holding us at bay and making us feel guilty. They have any number of ways of communicating to us that we have to warn them and cajole them and coax them and even bribe them. All of that is nonsense! The daughter had been clearly told what her chores were and what the time limits were. What Mother had never done before was to firmly enforce the rules.

And here is where the rubber meets the road in Reality Discipline. You will come to that moment when you have to enforce the rules and there will be tears and there will be accusations and chastisement. You can either shrink into a shell of guilt and permissiveness and relent or you can don your armor of authoritarianism. Neither will help.

What you have to do is what this mother did. She was calm but still determined. She was firm but still affectionate. Of course, she wasn't number one on her nine-year-old's popularity poll over that weekend. But she was more interested in teaching accountability than she was in copping out with permissiveness in order to get daugher to "like her." And that's what the teaching of accountability takes—sometimes we have to pull the rug out and let the little buzzards tumble.

Effective Reality Discipline is centered around the concept of controlling your emotions rather than having your emotions control you. This is obviously easier to say (or for me to write) than to do when the window is broken, or the vase has shattered on the floor. It's not always that easy to control one's emotions when little Clementine comes in late with a smart-alecky attitude, or you find four-year-old Cletus bathing his two-year-old sister in the toilet. Nonetheless, to blow up solves nothing. In fact, on those occasions when we do overreact and do not discipline in love, we owe it to our children to go to them and ask their forgiveness. This may be difficult, but it is a powerful tool to model the teachings of Christ to "forgive as the Lord forgave you" (see Ephesians 4:32 and Colossians 3:13).

In any situation, it is up to you, the parent, to evaluate what's going on and what the best approach will be. The key to interacting effectively with your children is to think before you discipline. I realize that is not always so simple, especially when Reality Discipline calls for decisive action and not stalling around. But in any situation, it never hurts to take a few moments to think through exactly what is going on and what needs to be done. By taking time out (if necessary, remove yourself or your children from the immediate situation), you decrease the probability of acting only in anger and you increase the probability of administering effective discipline.

Nine Ways to Be Your Child's Best Friend

In summary, here are nine principles to remember when using Reality Discipline to be your child's best friend:

1. The discipline should fit the infraction. For example, the child misuses his allowance. When he asks for something

extra before the week is out, you simply say, "Sorry, you will have to use your allowance and if you haven't any left, you will have to wait until Saturday."

2. Never beat or bully your child into submission. Remember, the shepherd's rod was used to guide the sheep, not to wale them.
3. Use action-oriented methods whenever possible.
4. Always try to be consistent.
5. Emphasize order and the need for order. Work comes before play, chores come before breakfast, and so on. This concept reinforces obedience and emphasizes that in all of God's kingdom, there is a need for order—order is important.
6. Always require your child to be accountable and responsible for his or her own actions.
7. Always communicate to your child that he or she is good, even though the behavior may have been irresponsible.
8. Always give your child choices that reinforce cooperation but not competition.
9. If spanking is necessary, it should be done when you're in control of your emotions. It should *always* be followed up with explanations for why the spanking was necessary, and those all-powerful words, "I love you and I care about you."

It's Simple, but Effective

I have had more than one parent say to me, "You're really asking an awful lot. I have difficulty disciplining my child with your methods."

I tell these parents that I empathize. Reality Discipline is a simple, straightforward approach, but it *is* difficult. It is not easy to be like the mother of the nine-year-old who failed to do her chores. The little girl neglected her responsibilities and could not go to her friend's house for the evening. She tried every trick she knew to make Mom feel guilty, but Mom hung in there. She was firm but still affectionate. She was understanding but still steadfast, *and she held her child accountable.*

There is nothing particularly unique about holding your child accountable. Many child-rearing specialists suggest this. But I like to believe that Reality Discipline is an especially effective way to do it because of the emphasis on being action-oriented, being willing to "pull the rug" with good humor but immovable determination. And it's worth it. Reality Discipline works! I see it work every day in my own home. I see it work in the families I counsel and speak to across the country. In Part Two of this book we will look at some specific problems, hassles, and concerns to see how Reality Discipline can improve and strengthen your relationship to your children—starting now.

Part Two

Using Reality Discipline in the Everyday Hassles

7

The Daily Battle

The following list of everyday hassles and concerns could be an endless one, but I have tried to select the topics about which I find parents continuing to ask questions. Many of these questions come to me through my newspaper advice column, "Parenthood Without Hassles—Well, Almost." Please remember that these suggestions are brief and space does not permit an exhaustive treatment of each problem or concern.

Also, the "answers" to these problems should not be considered guaranteed prescriptions for perfect parenting. Please don't use them as "the only way" to solve a particular problem. My work with hundreds of children and their parents over the years has shown me again and again that what works with one child may not necessarily be the answer for another. What I try to do in the following pages, however, is to give you some insight into using the principles of Reality Discipline in various situations.

Active Listening

Reality Discipline is based on action but it is also based on listening. When a problem arises, the very first thing you want to do is listen. Suppose your nine-year-old is stomping his feet and raging about his friend down the street, his teacher, or maybe his soccer coach. What are you to say? What could really help?

When you actively listen to your child, you don't correct him, lecture him, or threaten him. You simply let him know that you can see he's got a problem. You can say something like, "Hey, you look upset. Do you want to talk about it?"

If a child stomps out of the room and slams his bedroom door, you can make a pretty good guess that he doesn't want to talk about it right now. In a while, maybe half an hour, he'll come out and be contrite and willing to take up your offer.

When a child indicates he is willing to talk, your second step is to respond to his feelings. For example, the child may say, "You never let me do anything!"

An appropriate response from you that would let a child know you are aware of his feelings would be something like, "You're angry and upset with me." A nonproductive, unhealthy way to respond to a child's comment, "You never let me do anything," would be something like, "Don't you ever talk to me like that, young man. Don't you know who I am—I'm your mother!"

What should a parent say when the child says, "I can't do it, Mommy"? The parent who has not actively listened to the child's feelings would make a discouraging response, something along the lines of, "Of course you can do it. You just did the same thing last week." But when you are actively listening to feelings, an encouraging response might be, "It really seems hard for you."

It seems natural for most parents to feel that their first duty is to correct their child or lecture in some way in order to give the right solution or point out the right answer. As you cultivate the skill of active listening, you will do less and less lecturing and giving of right answers. You will resist the temptation to try to readily solve all the problems in your child's life. And you will do more and more empathizing— letting your child know that you understand how he feels and that you care about his feelings.

Anger

A common question I am asked at my Family Living seminars throughout the country is, "Should a parent ever get angry?"

Of course, parents should get angry! The question is, should we get angry at our child or at what our child does? When we begin to draw that fine line, we can see a much greater difference in the effect our anger will have.

Parents need the liberty of getting angry at what a child does. For example, suppose you have just cleaned the house and you find that your five-year-old has hauled out all his toys and left them in the living room. At a time like this it would be very appropriate for you to exercise your lungs and at the same time communicate how angry you are about the situation. The trick is in how you communicate your anger. You might use a statement like, "I feel so angry when I look at those toys scattered throughout the living room. I just spent two hours this morning cleaning up the house. I could just scream!"

Now that is an honest statement about how Mom might feel about a five-year-old's irresponsible behavior. Has Mom communicated that she doesn't love her child? No, she hasn't. She has simply sent him an "I" message that tells him she has angry feelings. She has not sent him any kind of "you" message that says, "You are a naughty child. I can't stand having you around. . . ."

Granted, it would be a good idea for Mom to sit down with her five-year-old (after he gets all of his toys picked up) and do a little more communicating. She could explain some of her feelings of anger and frustration. She could try to help him understand that she works hard to get the house straightened up and when he messes it up, it is very discouraging to her. All of this should be done with the five-year-old on Mom's lap, eyeball to eyeball, all the time holding and touching the five-year-old and reaffirming the fact that he is loved and accepted.

For more on handling anger and centering on the behavior and not the child, see "Communication," page 130.

Attention Seeking

The parent using Reality Discipline understands that children are always going to seek attention. From our earliest moments in life, we all seek attention in some shape or form. Infants, for example, learn they can get attention through crying. If the parents are always there to pick up the child at first peep, the child learns that as small as he might be he has a great deal of power and influence over adults.

As children grow, they begin to seek attention in positive ways. If they don't get attention and recognition through positive means, they turn to a myriad of negative methods that range from whining to dawdling behind, from tapping a pencil on the desk to combing hair at the dinner table.

Very early in life, children can develop faulty beliefs about themselves and others which, if not checked, will continue into adulthood. Examples of faulty thinking in a child's mind include: *I only count in life when I'm noticed. I only count in life when I can control or dominate or win.*

I say these are faulty ideas because they are simply not true. We do not count in life only when we can get the attention of others. As those who have been created by God, we already count. What we must do is meet our Maker on His ground and come to an understanding of His plan for us while we live on this earth.

The child's natural desire for attention is a critical reason Christian parents must take the time to train their children. We must take the time to enter each child's private world. We must get behind his or her eyes and see life as our son or daughter sees it.

As for how to get behind the eyes of your child, I suggest that you do a little "psychological guessing." Sit down with your child, look him right in the eye, and say, "You know, honey, I could be wrong, but as I watch you and your brother fighting, I get the idea you don't really hate your brother that much. It's just that you want a little more attention from me—that somehow you want to know that I really love and care about you. Is that what's really going on?"

Your child may not answer you directly, but watch his face. His expression will often reveal whether or not you have hit on what's really wrong. And once you do find out what's wrong, the child will feel better understood and the negative behavior will start being replaced by more positive behavior.

Bedtime Battles

A classic hassle occurs in many homes at bedtime. Children are often: a) resistant to going to bed; b) hard to get settled down once they are in the sack.

A key to handling the "Can I stay up a little longer?" ploy is to use the standard rule of Reality Discipline: direct and swift action. Do not argue or negotiate. Announce: "Bedtime at eight o'clock," or whatever you have set. Then stick with it.

With younger children, you may have an established routine to read a story and have prayers (see pages 144 and 145). With older children (seven and above) you may sometimes run into all kinds of stalling tactics (especially if a certain TV show is about to start). Do not argue, negotiate, and so on. Have a simple understanding: "Don't go to bed on time and your bedtime is even earlier for the next few nights." Or, "Don't go to bed on time and give up your favorite TV show for a week." The key is to not weaken or hesitate. Be pleasant and friendly but imitate General Ulysses S. Grant, Commander of the Northern Army during the Civil War. General Grant's motto was "unconditional surrender."

But suppose your little buzzards have gone quietly enough to their roosts for the night and after a few minutes you hear odd noises. (This is a typical problem when two children bunk together.) You can't concentrate on chatting with your spouse, on watching your program, or reading your paper. The thumps and squeals are just too loud. Once again the situation calls for action—direct and swift. What are your options?

You may or may not want to use a tactic I employed on one occasion. I recommend it as long as you use common sense and extreme caution. Our little girls, Holly and Krissy, were not settling down for the night. Before they knew it they were outside on the back porch in weather that was somewhat inclement (occasionally it does rain in Tucson). They stayed on the porch for exactly ninety seconds and then I let them back in. They went quietly to bed with no further delays or hassles.

If putting children outside for a brief time sounds too extreme or isn't practical, here are some other ideas: take both children from their bedroom and put them in another room such as the kitchen, the sewing room, possibly even the bathroom. Give them instructions to sit there until they can work out their problem. Under no circumstances are they to have available a TV, a radio, or some other toy or device with which they can amuse themselves. The idea is to sit on separate chairs and have a period of "time out" while they settle down.

Another approach is to separate the children. If one of them is obviously the culprit in the hassle, take him and put him in another room for a brief time. Again, he is to sit on a chair and go through a time-out period of five or ten minutes, until he can go back to bed quietly.

A final option is a spanking, but chances are a swat will not be necessary. Once you take action, your children will be much more likely to settle down. Wrestling and giggling in bed together is fun. Sitting in a room together is not fun. You can work out your own best approach to using action and not words to fight the bedtime battle. There are any number of strategies for moving in with positive discipline without playing the games your kids want you to play:

warnings, lectures, several trips to tell them to be quiet, and on and on.

Make clear to your children that bedtime is a must, not a negotiable option. They may protest, "But I'm not sleepy." Tell them, "Okay, you aren't sleepy, but it's still bedtime, so off to bed." Let them know that at the end of the day Mom and Dad need some moments by themselves to talk or do other things.

Comforting

Parents often face a child who is in distress, unhappy and crying over one problem or another. When does Reality Discipline say to go ahead and comfort and when should a different approach be used?

For example, what do you do when a child comes home crying over a bad report card? A healthy statement from Mom or Dad could be something like this: "You feel bad about your grades and you are discouraged. You're afraid that Mommy and Daddy will think less of you because you got bad grades." Obviously, an unhealthy response would be something like this: "You *ought* to be crying, with grades like that. I'd be ashamed to bring them home to my parents. In my day. . . ."

As soon as you use the words *in my day* you have turned off the communication valve in your child's mind. By showing disapproval of the bad grades, you have also only reinforced his fears and reason for crying.

When problems arise that cause your child to cry, here are some basic steps to take:

1. *Listen.* Listen carefully for what the child is saying and, more important, what the child is *feeling*.

2. *Respond to the child's feelings.* For example, in the healthy statement mentioned above the parent said, "You feel bad about your grades and are discouraged." This kind of comment tells the child that you know how he feels. The best thing you can show to your child is not sympathy

but empathy—letting your son or daughter know that you have a fairly good idea of how he feels and that maybe you've felt that way yourself sometimes.

3. *Never be afraid to touch your child.* Touching communicates that you understand and that you care. In many cases, a touch is worth many words.

Early in my career I learned that when a child feels under pressure he may cry. He often cries through previously learned behavior. He knows that when things get tough all he has to do is shed some tears and adults back off.

Several years ago, I was demonstrating some family counseling techniques to other teachers and counselors in a group situation. I had nearly one hundred people watching me work with a real family. I was working with a boy about eight years old and I could see he was about to cry. I didn't break stride in what I was saying. I simply reached over and touched his leg. The child sniffed a few times, pulled himself together, and we were able to continue the counseling demonstration.

I'm sure, however, that if I had stopped and shown concern over his teary eyes he would have started to shed real tears and the whole session would have had to come to a halt. Chances of getting the session going again would have been very slim.

By touching the child, however, I said to him, "Hey, I understand. I understand this is tough. I understand how you're feeling. You're not feeling real good right now but we're going to go on because we need to work this problem through."

Parents can often do the same thing with their children. A simple touch lets them know that you understand.

4. *Always look for alternatives.* In many cases a parent sees the child crying, hears the complaint, and is tempted to solve the problem quickly and easily from the adult point of view. Reality Discipline prefers to help the child solve his own problem, if possible. Think of alternatives that you can mention and urge your child to think of alternatives as well.

For example, suppose the family plans a picnic on Saturday, but everyone awakens to a torrential rainstorm. The picnic is ruined and your child starts to cry and carry on.

Hold the child close and show your own disappointment, but then ask the child if he can think of some alternatives. Perhaps you can have a picnic another day. If the child is young, waiting will not appeal too much. Perhaps you can have a picnic at home. (Be sure you have space to create a picnic setting in your family room!)

Whatever you do, do not chastise the child for his disappointment. But at the same time, do not simply give him the adult solution or reasoning such as, "Well, rainstorms happen. We'll just have to wait for another day."

5. *Give the child a choice.* After looking at all the alternatives, let the child choose—don't make the choice for him. When you make choices for your child, you are actually being disrespectful toward your child. Reality Discipline always trains the child to make his own choices in a responsible way.

6. *Never accept excuses.* When you begin to accept the child's excuses, you are really tempting him to always point his finger in some other direction than at himself. You encourage him to always find the fault elsewhere and not to face his own responsibilities.

7. *See your child's mistakes, not as defeats or frustrations, but as building blocks.* He learns from mistakes and so can you. Reality Discipline always teaches that the failures and mistakes of life are not negative but positive. They are important helps to learning how to improve and do better next time.

8. *Encourage commitment.* If you're working a problem through with your child, get a commitment from him to solve the problem through his own strength and efforts.

9. *Be ready to reevaluate the problem after the child tries to pick out a solution.* You may want to do this at several intermediate steps. Don't let the child flounder in failure. Always show your willingness to stand by him and give appropriate

help when needed. The first rule, however, is to let the child try to work it out himself.

I recall one occasion when Sande and I took all three of our children to the public library. Holly was in the fourth grade and needed some help with finding reference works, such as an encyclopedia. She started asking us to help her, but we gently suggested that she talk to the librarian and have the librarian show her how to find various reference works. Krissy and Kevin went their way to find the books they liked, while Sande and I browsed to find books that we were interested in.

Meanwhile, Holly did talk to the librarian and got the help she needed, and everything went beautifully. I believe, however, that if we had tried to help Holly find what she was looking for, it would have ended in some kind of hassle. Furthermore, she would not have learned how to use a library and how to get the librarian's help.

Communication

Without good communication, the action-oriented techniques of Reality Discipline will have limited results. The following are eight principles or rules for good communication with your children.

1. *Think before you speak.* Strive to accept your child as unconditionally as possible. Meet your child where he lives. Jesus always met people on their ground and dealt with them according to their needs. Always look for ways you can develop door openers with your children. Some of the simplest and best ones are, "Do you know, honey, I could be wrong, but. . . ." Or, "I could be way out in left field on this, but. . . ." These few words do much to put your children in a receptive mood. They are much more likely to listen to what you have to say because you are not coming on strong or in a threatening way.

2. *Stress the positive.* Make encouraging statements and compliments "second nature" in your conversation. Always

look for encouraging ways to interact with your children. Stressing the positive is just as easy as stressing the negative. Emphasizing the positive side takes no longer than the negative and the results are so much better. For example, your daughter is in a gymnastic meet and she scores very well in five events and poorly in one. You could say, "In those five events where you scored so well, you looked like you were having a great time and really enjoying yourself. You really did a good job. Congratulations." There is no need to even mention the event in which she did poorly. If she brings it up, you can say, "Yes, that one was tougher for you, but practice hard and you'll do better next time. I really like what you did in those other five events. I thought you were especially good on the balance beam. . . ."

3. *When you have to deal with the negative, do it in a positive, matter-of-fact way.* For one idea on how to handle this, see point 2 above and the suggested concern over doing poorly in one of the gymnastic events. Another example can be your four-year-old coming home with something that doesn't belong to him. It's obvious that he picked it up in your neighbor's yard. Do not berate him, lecture him, or carry on as if he were Public Enemy Number One. Simply say in a matter-of-fact way, "That doesn't belong to you, Buford. Let's take it back to the owner."

Then take Buford by the hand, walk him over to your neighbor's house, and have him return the item. Suggest to him that he say he is sorry he took it and that he won't do it again. On the way back home, say something like, "I'll bet you feel good about taking that back. Why don't we go play on the swings for a while?"

4. *Take time with your child.* Taking time with your child *communicates* that you really care. And I'm talking about special time—one on one—with each child each week. That's a tall order for most of us—but oh, so worthwhile. Mom and Dad should talk together about how they can help each other get away for one-on-one sessions with each of the

children. Yes, it will be a lot of trouble, but I repeat, it will make a tremendous difference.

5. *Always be aware that you don't have to like what your child does but you should always communicate that you love him and care about him.* Some simple things you can say include: "I want you to know that I'm very unhappy when you talk to me that way. I love you and care about you so much that I feel terrible when you speak like that. I know you are upset, but I don't think we should ever talk that way to each other—even when we're angry. What do you think?"

"Do you know why I yelled so loud for you to stop when you were running into the street? If a car hit you and killed you, I would be very, very sad. I love you too much to have anything like that happen."

When children misbehave, anger is a natural feeling. You do not have to be afraid to express your anger. But you must remember that your anger needs to be focused on the act or the behavior and not on the child.

6. *When you "blow it" with your children, ask their forgiveness.* This will accomplish two things. First, you will achieve much better communication with your children. Second, you will model how to ask forgiveness and help your children learn this difficult art.

When admitting your mistakes, start your statements with phrases such as, "I was wrong . . ." "I owe you an apology . . ." "I used poor judgment . . ." "I wasn't using my head. . . ." All of these phrases show the child your transparency and willingness to admit your imperfections. Do not worry that your child will lose respect for you under these circumstances. On the contrary, precisely the opposite will happen.

7. *Keep in mind that results aren't always evident over the short term.* Parenthood is for the long haul. It is a long-range investment. If your child doesn't always respond to the techniques of Reality Discipline, don't give up. You are going to discipline your child in one way or another, regardless of the

results, and you might as well be using a system that is based on Scripture (Ephesians 6:4) which will pay off in the long run.

8. *Ask for God's guidance daily, in your own life as well as in the lives of your children.* Let your prayer be that God's goodness and the joy of Christ will shine through your life in such a way that your children will see the reality of your personal relationship with the Almighty God.

Cooperation

Mothers in particular constantly ask me how they can get their children to cooperate more with doing chores, being on time, and so on. I believe Reality Discipline is the perfect tool for getting the child's attention and pointing out the need for cooperation in the home in a swift and direct manner. One basic approach is to teach the child that if he doesn't cooperate with you, you may not necessarily cooperate with him. This is the reality that he will always face in life, whether it be at school or later when he is grown up and has his own job and family.

I recall working with a mother whose little four-year-old would use whining, crying, and fussing as a way of keeping himself in control of situations at home. One afternoon, the mother asked her little boy to pick up his toys. It was a reasonable request. There weren't that many lying around and he knew exactly where they should go. But little Jimmy responded with, "They're too heavy."

At the time, Mom was fighting a deadline: she had a dentist appointment. She left the toys on the floor untouched and took the child with her to the dentist.

On the way home from the dentist, Jimmy began working on Mom for an ice cream treat. But as they drove by the ice cream stand, Mom turned to Jimmy and said quietly, "Honey, you can't have a treat today. You still have responsibilities left to do at home. I'm talking about your toys."

When they arrived home, there were the toys, lying where they had been left. Jimmy got the message. He picked up his toys and put them away.

In this simple incident we see Reality Discipline being demonstrated in several basic ways:

1. The mother loved the child so much that she wouldn't succumb to his every whim.
2. She would not be used or manipulated by the child. She was in authority over the child and not vice versa.
3. She did not "snowplow" the roads of life for her child by doing his work for him. If the mother had picked up the toys herself (which she could easily have done much faster), she would have been training him to be irresponsible.
4. The incident taught her son a basic lesson in cooperation: don't cooperate with Mom and Mom can't cooperate with you. The key point here, however, is not the "eye for an eye" concept as much as it is teaching the child that when you don't meet your responsibilities you can't have things your way.

Suppose the four-year-old had arrived home but still didn't want to pick up his toys. The mother could have invoked Reality Discipline in further ways by not allowing him to do anything until his chore was satisfactorily completed. There would have been no playing, no television, no snacks or treats. Reality Discipline stresses order, that A (the responsibility) comes before B (the reward or the treat).

Another important point is that the mother was quiet but firm. She did not shout at the child or verbally abuse him. You can try to shout or even beat your children into cooperating with you and at times you may think you are succeeding. But obtaining obedience through intimidation, nagging, and fear is not the way to teach cooperation. It is the way to teach your child to intimidate others as he gets older. With Reality Discipline, you are always seeking to respect your child as well as yourself. You are always trying to show your child that cooperation is a two-way street, not a one-way thoroughfare on which he does all the joyriding.

Courtesy

Another question I frequently get from mothers is, "How do I teach courtesy to my children? How can I teach them to say, 'Thank you,' 'You're welcome,' and, 'Please'?"

Obviously, courtesy is very close to cooperation, but you go at teaching courtesy in a different way from the the "eye for an eye" approach outlined above.

Almost everyone I know—other counselors, therapists, teachers, and parents—agrees that teaching courtesy has to begin at a very early age, so that it becomes second nature to a child to be courteous. I advise parents to get together with their spouses and decide on just what they want to teach by way of courtesy. Do you want to teach your child to say, "Yes sir," and, "No ma'am"? The other common amenities are undoubtedly on the list: "Thank you," "Please," "You're welcome," "May I. . . ."

We all have our basic ideas on these, and we can keep trying to drum them into our children. But while correcting them and eliciting the proper response from them is certainly part of teaching courtesy, there is little question that the real way to teach courtesy is to be courteous yourself. As parents model courtesy—to one another as well as to their children—they will teach it.

One way we teach courtesy in our home is by playing a game at dinner that I call "The Penny Game." Everyone, adults included, gets five pennies. The object is to catch someone who isn't using proper table manners (chewing with mouth open, napkin not on lap, elbows on table, reaching in front of someone, being boisterous). As dinner progresses, everyone is watching everyone else to see if they can catch them and get one of their pennies. For example, if my daughter sees me doing something wrong and calls me on it, I have to give her a penny.

This is an excellent game for children ten years old and under. Our children always love it. We've also had some good discussions that have come out of the game concerning why something is wrong and how it might be done better.

Suppose your child has said something discourteous to another person—child or adult. As I outlined in chapter 4, your best approach is to move in and "take the little buzzard by the beak." In other words, deal with the behavior then and there.

Do not reprimand your child in front of the offended party. Try to remove him from the room or at least go off a short distance and then speak to him. Gently but firmly tell him exactly what your feelings are about what he just said or did and why you feel that way. If the child is old enough (about three years or above), have him go back to the offended party and apologize. If the child refuses to do so, you may want to go to another form of discipline such as isolation: remove him from the group for a set period of time.

What you should always seek, if at all possible, is to have the child say, "I'm sorry," "Please forgive me," "Excuse me"—something that will convey to the offended person or persons that the child is sorry.

I repeat, the best way to teach this kind of courtesy is to practice it yourself. If you ever offend your child or your spouse, be willing to say, "I'm sorry," without hesitation.

Courtesy is a good discussion topic for a family at dinner, or perhaps at special times such as just before going to bed. Talk with your children about showing courtesies of one kind or another to each other. (You may learn something about what your children see as a "common courtesy" toward them!) Come up with specific ideas for showing courtesy to others and, more importantly, help your child understand how it makes a person feel when someone is courteous or discourteous.

Dangers of Life

How does a parent go about talking to children about the realities of living in a world where dangers are always present?

One simple technique you can use as you drive along with younger children is to point out the squashed skunks, bashed bunnies, flat cats, demolished dogs, and dented deer to dramatize what happens when "we don't look both ways."

If you have a swimming pool, be aware that children from three to six years old will often tell you they can swim when they really can't. To a child, "swimming" can mean splashing around in a pool. Give neighborhood children a short swimming test *before* they can enjoy full use of your pool. Always advise older children about the depth of the pool. It is wise to restrict diving by children.

I also suggest—with a *strong* note of caution—to occasionally read newspaper accounts about drownings to your children, particularly an account that deals with someone just about their age. Do not overdo this because you can misuse the fear factor. What you are interested in is creating a healthy respect for the dangers involved with swimming pools.

One danger to children that has become more prominent in recent years is abduction by strangers. A number of TV specials have covered cases of missing children and how they were abducted. How can you teach your child about "stranger danger"?

This is also a sensitive area because you don't want to unduly frighten your children. On the other hand, you want your children to be aware. I believe the realistic approach is to simply tell the children honestly and quietly that everyone in this world is not like Mommy and Daddy. There are many nice people but there are some very bad people. Let your children know that everything in life that happens to people isn't necessarily good. If you aren't careful, some bad things can happen to you.

Christian parents can let their children know that God will protect them as they learn to use their heads and the brains that God gave them to think with.

Talk with your children and even go through little scenarios about what to do if a stranger comes up and offers a ride. Make it a firm rule in your family that your children never accept rides from strangers and, quite obviously, never hitchhike. (When I was assistant dean of students at the University of Arizona, too often coeds were raped as a result of hitchhiking.)

Help your child think of statements a stranger might make in order to get him or her into a car. Ploys that child abductors use include: "Your dog has been hurt and I can take you to him." "Your mommy [or daddy] has been in an accident and they sent me to come and get you."

Point out to your children that if Mommy or Daddy were hurt, it certainly wouldn't be a stranger who would come and pick them up.

Also, give them alternatives and plans of action if they ever are stopped by someone. Tell them not to argue with the person or to even talk with him. Tell them to politely decline the invitation and to move on quickly. If the person appears to make any kind of advance, the child should be ready to run for the nearest help—to a house where there is a light on or someone can be seen through the window, for example.

Many neighborhood schools have enlisted the help of parents to provide emergency assistance to children in case of an incident. A large *E* (or other symbol) is displayed in the front window of homes to signify that these parents have the authority and willingness to help a child in an emergency. Talk to your child about the problem, go over the child's route to school, and identify such homes so that the child knows in advance where he can find help.

I agree that it is a sad commentary that we have to warn our children about such things, but the statistics on children who are abused, used, kidnapped, and even killed are rising every year. This is reality and you should take the time to help them understand. You are not trying to frighten them but to make them wise. If your child is old enough to be away from you, even for the briefest amount of time, help him learn how to become responsible and able to make quick decisions that will help him avoid harm.

Dinner Time Strategy

I touch on mealtime problems such as not eating in many other places in this book, but here I want to suggest a basic strategy for helping you apply Reality Discipline at that critical hour called "dinner time" when so many families seem to have a great deal of tension, stress, fighting, and upsets. Dinner time should be one of the more fulfilling, comforting, and strengthening times of the day, but in too many homes it is precisely the opposite. What can be done?

First, commit yourself to breaking the typical routine that you've probably been using. This is especially true in homes where the children resist eating, gripe about the food, and so on. Have everyone sit down to dinner, but don't bother to put food on the plates of your children. Let the children ask for things to be passed. Let them take exactly what they want. Do not nag or coax them to eat their vegetables or be sure to drink their milk.

Do not coax or remind your children to finish their meal. Don't waste your breath with stories about people in the Far East who are starving to death. Your children know there is no way to send them any of the particular food the family has been served for that meal. Some children are even aware that in many Eastern countries the people are eating fish and other healthy foods and are in better shape than many overfed and underexercised Americans.

In general, treat your children as if they are adults who are accountable for how much food they take and how much food they eat.

Then sit back and listen. See if the conversation around the table changes. Talk about subjects of interest to you and to them. If they don't want to tell you what happened at school, don't worry about it. But do everything you can to maintain a casual, relaxed situation.

Be aware that your children will soon catch on to what you are trying to do and they will counterattack. They will lay traps and try to embroil you in controversy over whether they're eating or not eating. Just stay calm but firm. Don't get involved with what they are eating. Above all, enjoy your own meal.

For those parents who are both working, I add the following strategic suggestions. As I deal with families in which Mom has to work, I find that in many homes the children are expected to have dinner partially started, to have the table set, the garbage taken out, and so on. I believe children should be involved in doing chores in every home, but I especially applaud their involvement in the home where Mom and Dad are both working. When both parents have to work and Mom has little time to prepare dinner, assigning responsibilities to the children is a beautiful opportunity to put the principles of Reality Discipline to work.

But what if it doesn't seem to work? What if Mom and Dad come home and see that the table is not set, the garbage isn't out, and dinner is unstarted? The children are busy—off with their friends, repelling the latest Atari attack, and so on. What does Reality Discipline say at a moment like that? It says to use action, not words, but not the type of action you might think. Do not move in to invoke logical consequences. Do not do any reminding or coaxing, bribing or threatening, or blowing up. Simply sit down and read the paper. Relax and wind down from your busy day.

Sooner or later, one of your children will come in and ask

the obvious questions: "When is dinner going to be ready? What's for dinner?"

Here is the opportunity for Mom or Dad to say in a low-key manner: "When the kitchen is ready for operation, dinner will be started. Right now, the kitchen looks as if no one is interested in dinner tonight. We can't prepare dinner in a messy, unsanitary kitchen."

This kind of response teaches your children that order is important. If they cannot help keep the house in an orderly condition, dinner will not be prepared.

Oh, yes, be sure you do not let your children "have dinner" by grabbing the nearest box of snack crackers or bag of chips and starting to munch away in front of the TV set. Let them know that no eating will be done until the responsibilities that were supposed to have been met are completed.

Encouragement

As I deal with parents, I see many of them who find it difficult to grasp the difference between giving their child encouragement and giving praise. After all, many books tell parents to compliment and praise their children often. Indeed, one of the problems in too many homes is that too many children never get any compliments or praise to speak of; they are usually criticized or told what they didn't do rather than what they did well.

I understand the motivation behind admonishing parents to praise their children, but I prefer to stress the need for encouragement rather than praise. It is difficult to understand; nonetheless it is true: praise can be very discouraging. In the ultimate sense, only God is worthy of praise. People need encouragement, not praise.

Encouragement centers on a person's efforts, improvement, sense of responsibility, tenacity, and appreciation for progress. Examples of encouraging words to your children are these:

"I'm sure you can handle it."

"I'm glad to see you enjoy learning."

"How thoughtful of you—the kitchen looks great!"

"Now you're getting it!"

"You looked as if you were having a great time in the game today."

"It looks as if that extra practice really paid off for you—congratulations!"

"How do you feel? You've come a long way."

By contrast, statements of praise sound like this:

"My, you're a good boy."

"Mommy is so proud of you, dear. You did so well in the recital tonight."

"You ate all your dinner. What a good girl! Now you can have dessert."

"Three *A*s and a *B!* That makes me so happy. Now next time, let's get that *B* up to an *A!*"

"Your behavior was great at the scout meeting tonight. Here's five dollars to show you how much it meant to me."

As I mentioned in chapter 5, in *Parenthood Without Hassles—Well, Almost,* I included what I called "A Child's Ten Commandments to Parents." All of these "commandments" are written in the words of a young child to his parents. One of them says: "I need your encouragement, but not your praise, to grow. Please go easy on the criticism; remember, you can criticize *the things I do* without criticizing *me.*"

I encourage all parents to be aware of what they are saying to their children. Are your remarks more in the form of praise or are you learning how to encourage instead? The difference is subtle but vitally important. Praise can actually defeat and deflate a person's sense of self-worth, particularly a child's. Praise suggests *qualified* love. It triggers in a child's mind the questions, *Am I loved and praised because I got good grades or cleaned the kitchen? What would happen if I didn't do those things?*

Fears

Children—particularly the very young, under six years of age—frequently have fears. Fears come in all sizes and shapes: nightmares, fears of the dark, and others. Most parents find that their children's fears center around nighttime, going to sleep, and being in the bedroom alone.

There are some very obvious ways to help your child conquer fears: night-lights and leaving the hall light on among them. Every parent should be aware that *most* fears resulting in nightmares, night terrors, and abnormal thoughts and feelings are a direct result of allowing children to watch violence on television. Parents must be acutely aware of the potential long-term damage that can result from allowing their children to watch violent or frightening programs and films. Doctor James Dobson cites a study at Cornell University which demonstrated that middle-class fathers of preschool children spent an average of thirty-seven seconds a day with their children. In contrast, it showed that children watched television fifty-four hours per week!

One of the best ways to help your children with their fears is to talk about your own fears. Most of us, as children, had fears of one thing or another. It's good to share your own experiences with your child. Tell how you recognized and handled certain fears in your own life. Never criticize or reprimand your child for having fears. Whatever you do, don't make fun of him, no matter how amusing a certain remark he made might be. Help your child understand that everyone has fears and that with help and encouragement, he can overcome what is making him afraid.

Keep in mind, however, that a child may use fear in the same way he might use remorse—as a ploy or a manipulative tool. Children are masters at needlessly involving Mom and Dad in their lives. They want to monopolize their parents and will go to great lengths to do so. At a very young age, they can become masters at this art.

One of the suggestions I make to parents of young children (under five) is that bedtime itself should include a built-in routine. As the child gets tucked in there can be a prayer time plus a story time, or perhaps you may want to play a recording. Make it clear that there is one story or one playing of a record and then the door is closed and it is not to open again.

Now, a powerful child will test you on that. He'll test you with screaming, yelling, and other carrying on. I have counseled parents whose children have screamed for two, three, and four hours at a time. This can be tremendously irritating and eventually the parent may weaken. But it doesn't do any good to hold out for an hour and forty-five minutes and then finally give in and go see what's wrong. All we have taught the child is that if he screams long enough and hard enough, sooner or later Mommy or Daddy will give in.

If you are having trouble establishing the right kind of routine to get your child asleep, one technique you might use is the tape recorder. Try to get one that will shut off automatically after the tape is over. There are many good but inexpensive tape recorders available, and they usually shut off automatically. Ask about this feature before buying one.

As for tapes you can play, see what is available at your Christian bookstore. Many tapes come complete with a storybook.

Whatever you try, remember these basic principles:

1. Create a routine the child can count on.
2. Use a record or tape recording as the last step in getting the child to sleep.
3. Do not open the child's door for any reason once the child is tucked in.
4. If the child gets out of bed for any reason, he will have to tuck himself back into bed. In time, this will reinforce his staying in bed.
5. Your tucking in and prayer time can be a wonderful opportunity to talk with your child about the events of the day (his or yours). *Do not hurry while you are tucking your*

child in and praying with him. This is your daily opportunity to communicate your love to your child at a critical moment. Do not rush off to catch the first act of a play or the first hymn in a service. Your child is more important.

Fighting

Many parents I talk to seem to believe it's impossible to have children who don't fight. Yet I also know of families in which fighting among siblings is minimal. If we understand the dynamics of why children fight, we can make some inroads in correcting the situation.

Realize first of all that when two of your children fight, they are cooperating with each other. It seems odd to call fighting an act of cooperation, but that is exactly what is happening. It is extremely difficult to get a fight going with only one person. As the old cliché puts it, "It takes two to tango." The other person has to say just the right word, or use just the right facial expression or gesture, to get the fight going and to keep it going.

I have found that the best way to handle fighting is to give the children what they seem to say they want. If they want to fight, let them fight. I always tell parents, however, that they have the right to say where the children can fight and under what conditions. If the children fight, it cannot interfere with the peace and welfare of others in the home.

When two children start fighting, it is best to guide them (if they're little, carry them) to a room elsewhere in the house, or possibly to the backyard. Give them instructions to continue fighting until they have worked out their problem. Leave them to their "fight." In most cases, when you give children permission to fight, they won't. They merely stand and look at each other. One might say, "All right, you start it." And the other one replies, "No, *you* start it."

What usually happens is that neither of them starts it because they don't want to fight that badly. Their fighting, for the most part, was designed to get the parents needlessly involved in their hassles. The sooner parents learn to stay out of their children's hassles the sooner they will teach their children greater responsibility and accountability. Many schoolteachers tell me that when they find children fighting they solve the problem this way: they give both children boxing gloves, take away their audience, put them in a gym, and tell them to go ahead and box it out. But in these situations the children seldom fight either. Children usually fight for attention. They want an audience—their peers or, if they are at home, their parents. Take away the audience and the fight usually stops.

There are, of course, exceptions to every rule or general principle. There are times when one child may pick a fight with another who is totally outmatched in size and strength. I know of one mother who found her twelve-year-old choking his nine-year-old brother, who was rapidly turning blue. That was the day the boys got separate bedrooms!

Many times the fighting is not physical but verbal. There is a lot of bantering back and forth. Then it turns into name-calling and finally into a shouting match. If this happens at the dinner table, just excuse the children and tell them to leave the table and go to another part of the house or outside. If they are more interested in name-calling and arguing than they are in eating, they may do it elsewhere. It is usually a good idea to escort them to wherever you want them to go and then give them instructions to stay in the room or outside in the yard until they've worked out their problems. Only when they have worked out their problems and are willing to behave quietly may they rejoin the others at the dinner table.

Always be sure to let reality be the teacher. If dinner is over by the time the children get back, there will be no more food and no special meal for them. They will have missed their meal in order to engage in their fight. Reality has moved in to stress the need for social order and treating one another respectfully. If they can't get their disagreement settled before dinner is over, dinner is over anyway. It's a little like not getting your act together in the morning and running to catch the bus, only to see it pull away just as you round the corner.

Reality Discipline stresses the realities in this world, and the realities say that certain things are done during a time frame. If you don't make one time frame, you have to wait for the next one. If you miss one bus, you must wait for the next one. If you miss one meal, you wait for the next one.

Fighting—verbal or physical—often occurs while the family is traveling in the car. In cases like this, it's best to pull over and stop. If possible, get out of the car and go for a short walk and allow the children to continue fighting. (They will soon stop.) If it is not safe to leave the car, simply tell the children that they can continue fighting but the car will not move until they are through.

The key here is to be calm and not get angry yourself. If the children are on the way to participate in one of their own activities (Little League baseball or football, music lesson, and so on), it will be all the better. There will be a natural consequence for their misbehavior.

I believe parents are being responsible when they decide not to operate a motor vehicle while a fight is in progress. Again, the message to the children is, "Well, you can fight, but I'm not going to continue until the fighting has stopped." The fighting usually stops in a minute or less. If the fighting does not stop, simply have the courage to turn around and drive back home.

In every case, your goal is to not encourage fighting. You want your children to see that fighting is not a good way to solve problems. You want your children to learn:

1. Fighting gets no payoff from Mom and Dad, not even a negative one.
2. If I fight, I can get hurt.
3. If I fight, I may not go to Little League, the park, or other places.

Remember, there is no way (mine or anyone else's) to eliminate rivalry between siblings. All you can hope for realistically is to minimize it. Conflict in the home, particularly among siblings, is natural. As you help your child learn to solve his conflicts in a positive way, you build his psychological muscles for dealing with the realities of life.

Forgetting

Does your child seem to suffer temporary losses of memory from time to time? I'm not talking about amnesia. I'm talking about those times when you ask him to do a particular task and later he responds by saying half apologetically, "Oh, I forgot."

What's important here is to realize *why* your child keeps forgetting things—particularly things you've asked him to do. Is the child getting a payoff from the forgetting? I'm not talking about an extra allowance. I'm talking about letting the child get away with another kind of manipulative ploy.

If you ask the child to do something and he forgets and then you go ahead and do the task for him, he is getting the payoff he is looking for. You have reinforced his forgetting habit and at the same time you have weakened the child in some serious ways. For one, you weaken his self-confidence. You also weaken his ability to think and to remember things that are important. In the long run, you weaken his ability to be accountable and responsible.

Whenever parents complain to me about their child's "forgetfulness," I immediately urge them to not let forgetting be an excuse for not doing a task. Reality Discipline accepts no excuses. (You may accept reasons in extenuating circumstances but not continual excuses that fall into patterns.) Even if it's difficult and you feel like you are being "mean," remember that in the future your child will be working for people who will not accept excuses or apologies because he "forgot."

So, always stand on the basic principle. If your child's been asked to do something and then "forgets," make him do it anyway. If it means missing his favorite TV program, being late for where he is going (including school), or having to be inconvenienced in any number of other ways, so be it. Life will not tolerate your child's excuses and neither should you.

Getting Up in the Morning

From what I hear in counseling sessions and through questions I get in the mail, it would appear that many American homes are battle zones—especially in the morning. It seems to be a knock-down-drag-out battle to get little Buford out of bed and ready on time for school. Whenever mothers or dads approach me with the "How do I get my child to get up?" problem, I remind them of one of the basic principles of Reality Discipline: *you can't make another person do anything;* you guide him or her in such a way that reality makes him do what he needs to do.

So, the best way to proceed with the "can't get 'em up in the morning" crisis is to remove yourself from all responsibility. In other words, declare an armistice over the battle zone. You are not going to bug your child about getting up anymore.

Am I suggesting that you even allow the child to sleep in past the beginning of school hours? Absolutely. Let reality get your child up. After you have tried unsuccessfully a number of times to get your child up, simply refuse to cooperate. Refuse to be used as a human alarm clock. Tell your child he will have to figure out some way to get himself up. He will have to make some appropriate decisions about how he is going to get his body out of bed and off to school in the morning. If he fails to get to school, all kinds of reality will set in. The main reality will be big trouble with his teachers. True, the teachers may call you, but you simply will pass the message on to your child. Don't let the teachers intimidate you, put you on a guilt trip, or in some other way force you to go back to being a human alarm clock.

One obvious solution to the child's problem is that he get his own alarm clock. Provide him with one and show him how to set it. If he forgets to set his clock, he suffers the same kind of consequences that you do when you forget to set yours for an important date or meeting.

You may want to involve the child's teacher, or teachers, at school in your plan. Call the school and say that your child is going to be late because he has overslept and that you believe it would be a good idea if there were some definite consequences for his tardiness. When Buford arrives at school, his teacher might say, "Buford, I see you're late but you're very lucky. You're going to be able to make up that twenty minutes you missed this morning by staying in at recess and doing some work while the rest of the kids go out and play."

Granted, calling Buford's bluff and letting him sleep in and be late for school is not an easy task or prospect. It can cause you anything from embarrassment to inconvenience. For example, you may have to drive Buford to his school because the bus will not be available by the time he's ready. (On the other hand, if the school is anywhere within walking distance, let Buford be the one who's inconvenienced—let him walk.)

Winning the "can't get 'em up in the morning" battle may be tough, but if you persevere for a few days or possibly a week or two, it will pay off. The choice is yours: you can remain a human alarm clock and take the responsibilities that really belong to your child, or you can turn those responsibilities over to him and let him be accountable for getting up in the morning.

Please note, however, that you could be one of those lucky parents who has a child who gets up at first call in the morning with no particular problems. If you are so blessed, please ignore all my advice about buying alarm clocks and continue in your bliss. Later, as the child grows older, he may want his own alarm clock, but it will be for his own convenience not as a disciplinary measure.

Homework

Getting children to do their homework is a problem as early as third grade in many school systems across the country. Most teachers I talk to tell me that if the child is efficient at all with the use of his time, he can get most of his homework done during free time while still at school. Of course, many children prefer to play or fritter away the minutes in other ways, and they have to bring the homework home.

And there's where the battle starts. For parents who are involved in their child's homework problems, I suggest several basic steps:

1. *Remembering a basic Reality Discipline principle, they do not try to "make" their child do his homework.* What they should do is try to provide an environment conducive to study time. In some homes that is all Mom and Dad really need to do. Some children are self-directed enough to want to do a good job on their homework and with a little cooperation from Mom or Dad, they finish it in good order.

If possible, provide a special study room, but if this is a luxury that isn't available, the child's bedroom is usually the place he will study. He should have a desk and some space where he can spread out his books and papers.

It is also a good idea to allot certain times for children to do their schoolwork. After dinner, from 6:30 to 8:00 P.M., Mondays through Thursdays, would be appropriate for the fourth through the eighth grade. Younger children would benefit from the same schedule but with less time, perhaps 6:30 to 7:00 or 7:15 P.M. Of course this will vary according to family circumstances.

Mom can cooperate by being mindful that while little Buford is studying, she should make a concentrated effort to be as quiet as possible. Running the vacuum cleaner, for example, isn't going to help get the homework done.

2. *Another critical point that many parents have to consider is that they should not do the child's homework for him.* Some people chuckle at the concept of a parent doing the child's homework, but I have known many parents who have done exactly that—on a regular basis. (Some of the worst offenders are parents who are also teachers. After dinner they turn the home into a pseudoschoolhouse.)

I strongly urge parents to back off and refuse to get involved in homework to any great degree. If a child asks for help with his work occasionally, that's another matter. But everyone has to understand that "occasionally" means exactly that. If you don't watch it, you will soon be sucked into a situation where you spend most of your evening hours through the week with your child's schoolwork. If that has been happening to you, something is wrong. Get together with the child's teacher or counselor and talk about it. Make a commitment to stay out of your child's schoolwork and to assist the teacher in every way you can in getting the child to do his own work.

This can sometimes be difficult for parents because they have a natural inclination to want to help the child (who may be having some genuine difficulties). And, there is always the factor of parental pride—the embarrassment of having little Buford push *C*s and *D*s when the parent knows he could help him get *B*s and maybe even an *A*.

But the realities of life demand that your child learn to do things on his own. It is much better for your child to earn a *C* than to have you help get a *B+* or an *A*.

So, my rule of thumb is: some help, yes; a lot of help, no; continual help, never! For example, if your child comes and asks you to drill him on his spelling words, go ahead and do so. That takes a relatively short amount of time and falls into the category of real help and not just doing his work for him. And, it helps show your child that you are interested in what he is doing.

3. *But suppose your child just isn't getting into his homework.* Suppose you have provided the study space and have made every effort to keep the house quiet, and your child still isn't getting the homework assignments done. Your next step would be to create some logical consequences (see chapter 6). The best way to use logical consequences is by talking with your child and letting him help set the consequences.

For example, if his homework is not done and his grades are not *C* or better, he will not be able to go out to play after school or after supper. He may not engage in extracurricular activities or sports such as Little League. I repeat, talk with your child about what he thinks would be fair and work out something that sounds reasonable to both of you.

Also remember that the grades your child gets are *his* and not *yours.* Be sure to talk to your child about his grades. While looking over a poor report card you might want to comment, "I'm very sorry to see that you don't enjoy learning." This would be an honest comment but would not be critical or demeaning.

If your child seems to make little improvement, be patient. Some children do not do well in school in certain grades and then improve a great deal later on. As a Christian parent you have been given authority and responsibility by God to train your child correctly. Always teach your child the following order of responsibilities and priorities:

1. God
2. Parents
3. Home and family
4. School
5. Extracurricular activities

Love

This suggestion almost seems unnecessary, yet I deal with parents all the time who find it difficult to tell their children,

"I love you." Perhaps these parents were brought up in homes where they weren't told they were loved and it is difficult for them to share their own intimate thoughts and feelings with their own children. But if Reality Discipline is to work for you the way it can, you must be able to communicate your feelings of love.

We have three children, and I can't remember a day in any of their lives, when I was in contact with them at all, when I didn't tell them, "I love you." And not only do I tell them, I show them. I can think of three ways to communicate love to a child:

1. Discipline the child. I'm not talking about punishment—I'm talking about giving the child the loving correction he or she needs at the time it is needed.
2. Touch your children. Hug them, pat them. The power of touch is incredible!
3. Show interest in what your child is interested in. So many children live their own lives while Mom and Dad, it seems, live theirs.

I've already mentioned the survey made by family counselor Craig Massey, who found that 79 percent of the twenty-two hundred children from Christian homes which he surveyed, felt unloved. One survey doesn't necessarily make a total case, but nonetheless to find 79 percent of *any* group feeling unloved is mind-boggling, and when the survey is done among Christian homes, it is even more mind-boggling. How can this be? Why is it that in homes where the parents supposedly have a relationship to God in Christ, and know something of God's love, children feel unloved? I think one of the basic answers has to be that parents simply do not know how to communicate their love. They find it hard to use the words; they find it hard to touch; and they also find it hard to let their children grow up and learn to make their own decisions. It may seem paradoxical, but one way to communicate your love to your child is to give your child the freedom to make decisions. And, give your child the freedom to fail. When the failures come, that's the time to really say, "I love you," and to show it with hugs and pats and smiles.

Lying

The parents I know want their children to tell them the truth. Christian parents are particularly concerned about lying and why their children sometimes resort to this kind of dishonesty. Lying usually falls into two basic patterns:

1. *Some children lie out of wish fulfillment.* This kind of lie expresses a simple childlike fantasy. Very young children sometimes fantasize about imaginary friends, seeing Rudolf the Red-Nosed Reindeer, and so on. These "lies" are usually isolated incidents and not something to be greatly concerned about.

2. *The reason most lies are told, however, is out of fear.* No matter how much a child is loved and accepted, he is afraid that if he tells his parents the truth about some misbehavior, something unpleasant will happen. He will be punished in some way. At the very foundation of his fears is the fear that if he tells the truth he will not be loved. The child sees himself as having to be perfect in order to deserve love.

Fibs or little white lies are often spontaneous attempts to cover up small imperfections. If a parent is authoritarian, it will set the stage for more lying. The child of the authoritarian parent is often defeated by unrealistic expectations (not to mention fear). Something else you can do is share your own imperfections with your child. Help him or her realize that all of us are imperfect in one way or another. One time Krissy, my nine-year-old, came to me in tears because she realized she had lied regarding a telephone call for me. Actually it was my fault. Without thinking I had told her to tell someone I wasn't home, when in fact I was, but was shaving in the bathroom.

Mothers sometimes tell their children they don't have

time to bake cookies or make lemonade. In reality they have time but they don't have the energy. It is better to be honest and say, "I'm too tired," or even, "I'm not in the mood right now."

Most parents I deal with know something about having their children lie or at least shade the truth (white lies). In many cases, parents would settle for having the child tell the truth and that would be the end of it. There would be no punishment or any particular form of discipline. Unfortunately, there are times when the child has to be held accountable for lies and some kind of consequence has to be invoked. When this does happen, be sure to make it clear to the child that while he has lied and you have to invoke a consequence, you still love him very much and you hope he will not feel he has to lie in the future.

Parents can encourage their children to stop lying with the following strategies:

1. *Always trust your child.* Give him the opportunity to tell the truth. When he does tell the truth, thank him and try to go on from there. If a consequence is necessary, carefully explain why, but point out that the truth is always better than the lie.

2. *Always seize every opportunity to show children why lying never pays.* One lie always has to lead to another. I always like to tell my children, "If you don't lie, you don't have to have such a good memory." The liar is always having to remember what he said to whom, and when, and how he can cover up his last lie with another one.

Mistakes

I'm not talking about mistakes by your kids. I mean the ones *you* make. Now what does a parent do when he makes a mistake? I know it sounds easy to lay out step-by-step ways to solve problems with your children, but I also know the feelings of frustration and failure when things don't work out perfectly. I know what it's like to have my plans and convictions and motivations go astray. Life is not perfect, and neither are we.

I think of the time my daughter Krissy was six years old and just learning to ride a two-wheeler bike. She got to the point where I felt she really had the ability to ride by herself without any support or extra help. She would take a couple of steps, jump on her bike, pedal a couple of times, and then jump off. It seemed that all she needed was the confidence to stay on and keep going.

So, one Saturday morning, *Dad* decided that today Krissy would learn to "really ride a bike."

My arbitrary decision that this was Krissy's day to learn what I wanted her to learn was my first mistake. I got her out in the street in the residential area where we live. I walked her along with both hands on the bike. Then she pedaled a little bit and we went up a hill and began to come down the other side. Now she was pedaling gently along and I was trotting along next to her, still balancing the bike. I had already let go for a few seconds to make sure she could balance properly and she was doing nicely. We went a few more feet and I made the decision (without checking with Krissy) to let her go the rest of the way down the hill all by herself. As I let go of her, her speed accelerated, she lost control, and veered off the street straight into a cactus bush. If you haven't noted before, we live in Tucson, Arizona, which grows some of the meanest cactus bushes in the west. Poor little Krissy went tumbling off straight into the bush and we spent quite a while picking stickers out of her little six-year-old body.

Of course, I hurt more than she did, but that didn't make Krissy feel any better. And it was a long time before Krissy got back on that bike—at least a good year.

Of course, she learned a couple of things from her experience with letting Dad teach her to ride a bike:

1. Stay away from two-wheeler bikes—they're dangerous.
2. Stay away from Dad—he's even more dangerous!

I did learn quite a bit that day, however. I learned that I had interrupted Krissy, who was learning to ride a bike in her own way and at her own speed. With all my motivation to be a good guy and a helpful daddy, I had moved in and tried to force her to go too far too fast. I tried to make her learn at my speed and it had ended in disaster.

I tell you that illustration to help you understand two things:

1. *Never force your child to do more than he or she is able to do.* When using Reality Discipline, it is possible to go over the line and in trying to make a child accountable and responsible, we can push the child beyond his capabilities at the time.

2. *Hold your child accountable, but don't apply unnecessary pressure.* How do you know when you are applying unnecessary pressure? There is no absolute and guaranteed way to know—you will just have to tune in to your child and communicate (see "Communication").

3. *Using Reality Discipline cuts both ways.* You always want the child to understand what reality is, but you also need to understand reality—especially the reality of your child's abilities, fears, and weaknesses. In short, Reality Discipline is always ministered with a good dose of love.

Nagging

Parents are often caught in a bind. They find themselves having to remind their children to do or not do certain things. The parent does the reminding while all the child hears is "nagging."

Reality Discipline has an answer for the problem. Simply stop doing all that reminding.

Parents look at me as if I've lost my mind when I make that suggestion. They ask a very logical question: "What's wrong with reminding a child? Doesn't everyone need a reminder once in a while?"

Yes, I'm sure most human beings need to be reminded of

things now and then, but the problem with parents is that they have let it get too out of hand. The pattern, in many homes, is that Mom and Dad constantly remind or coax the children to do things they are expected to do on a regular and routine basis. I tell parents to stop this pattern of reminding and coaxing. When you continue to remind and coax your child to do things that he knows he is supposed to do, you are teaching him to be irresponsible.

For example, when you constantly have to coax or remind a child to come to dinner, you are simply teaching him that the first call doesn't matter. He can continue watching TV, playing, or building his model airplane and Mom will continue to call three or four more times. When the decibel level gets up to a certain intensity, then he knows he'd better come.

All of this is very hard on everyone. The choice is clear: you can train your children up to respond the first time they are asked to do things, or you can train them to not listen to the first request or warning and simply go on their merry way until they cause a problem.

So, how do you apply Reality Discipline to the reminding and nagging problem? Let your children know that you are going to tell them things only once. You are not going to be disrespectful to them by communicating that you think they are so stupid they cannot understand what you say the first time you say it. Tell them you are not going to repeat things over and over again. If they do not come or do not heed the first time, you will move in with actions and not words. Let them know what the consequences will be if they do not come the first time (for example, if called to dinner and they don't come, they don't get dinner). And then back up what you say.

I repeat, the choice is yours. You can deal with your children in a mentally healthy way or in an unhealthy way. To continually remind, nag, and coax is unhealthy for everyone concerned.

Not Eating

We've already touched on this in earlier chapters. My work with parents and children tells me there are far too many hassles in the American home every night at the dinner table. It also happens at breakfast and lunch, but dinner seems to be the special time when little Rufus and little Zelda decide they are not going to eat.

My basic premise is that when a child doesn't want to eat, bribing and rewarding aren't going to work. Neither does "playing airplane," which went out twenty years ago. (In case you don't know how to play airplane, you say, "Open the hangar door," and on and on.)

Reality Discipline has a simple approach to dealing with the child who does not eat. You simply hold him accountable for his choice. Remove the food from the plate, dump it in the garbage, and excuse the child from the table. This works with ten-year-olds as well as three-year-olds.

Actually, removing the food and excusing the child is the easy part. The hard part comes when you have to back up your actions by refusing the child any more food for the evening. Here is where you have to let the child experience the reality of being hungry because he chose not to eat dinner. If you call little Rufus's bluff, take away his food, and tell him, "Dinner is over for you. Run along and play," you can be sure that a couple of things will soon happen:

1. *Rufus will be back shortly, whining and fussing that he is hungry.* At this time you simply say, "I'll bet you are. Could it have anything to do with the fact that you didn't eat your dinner, Snookums?"

2. *The other thing that is very likely to happen is that the child will eat a huge breakfast the next morning.* I know some of you are probably thinking, *What? Let my child miss a meal?* Your pediatrician will tell you that a child will not die if he misses a meal—and that missed meal will do much to teach your child what reality is all about.

When your child wants to play the "I'm not hungry"

game, it's important that you don't fall into the same old trap that some of our parents did when we were kids. No bribing, rewarding, cajoling, pleading, threatening, screaming, or spanking. Give the child the right to make his own decision and then hold him accountable.

Oh, yes, if it goes too hard against your grain to dump the food in the garbage, simply put it in the refrigerator for leftovers.

Peer Group

As your children get older, the peer group starts to make its presence felt. I find peer-group pressure starting with children as early as first and second grade.

In order for parents to fulfill their mission, they must realize that their children want to belong. Every child is going to belong somewhere. He has two basic choices: he can identify himself with his family or he can identify himself with his peer group—the other kids on the block or at school. Rest assured, however, that your child will belong somewhere.

The challenge for parents is to communicate daily to their children that they belong in the family. Feelings of belonging are one of the key building blocks of self-esteem. If your child feels he is building self-esteem at home, he is much less likely to be influenced by his peer group. Here are some simple things you can do to make your child feel, "I belong. Mom and Dad really love me."

1. *Let your children have a say in planning family activities, outings, trips, and vacations.* Solicit their opinions on what they would like to do. Be willing to meet them halfway.

2. *Ask for their opinions about problems you—the parents and other members of the family—are facing.* These problems might be spiritual, financial, or emotional. When you ask for their ideas, you are saying, "I value your opinion. You are worthwhile and important in this family."

3. *I believe we also tell children they belong when we give them work to do within the family structure.* Don't assign

chores as if they are distasteful tasks everyone is stuck with. Help your children see that doing chores well is a way of taking pride in how the house looks. Granted, the appearance of the house won't be too high on their priority list until perhaps a few years later. But as they start having friends come over—particularly when they reach junior high school level and start interacting more with the opposite sex—they may make a radical improvement. Indeed, little Festus may turn into a junior-high version of the "white tornado" to make the house presentable for visits by his friends.

4. *Let your child test the system* (*the family's rules*) *and be willing to engage in give-and-take.* Eradicate from your vocabulary such phrases as, "You do it because I said so," or, "As long as you live here, you'll do it our way." Instead, be willing to reason with your child and explain *why* you believe and do *what* you believe and do. By taking time to give reasons for rules, you are saying to the child in still another way, "I value you as a person. I am paying you the compliment of treating you like someone who can think for himself."

If you want to do some further reading in the area of peer-group pressure, I suggest the following three books. Each author takes a little different slant, but all three books give key insights on the realities of what your child is facing already or will very soon be facing from his peers, and how you can make him feel more secure and accepted at home:

Preparing for Adolescence by James Dobson, published by Vision House

Smart Girls Don't, and Guys Don't Either by Kevin Leman, published by Regal Books

What Teenagers Wish Their Parents Knew About Kids by Fritz Ridenour, published by Word Books

Potty Training

Toilet training your child is one task that probably requires more Reality Discipline for you than it does for your child. We all know the lady whose child was potty trained at ten months, or fourteen months. In many cases, the child hasn't been potty trained—the mother has. As long as she remembers to put the child on the potty, she probably experiences few accidents. Of course, there are exceptional children who do learn to use the potty at a very young age, but there is no rule of thumb. There is no magic day when every child should take his postgraduate course in bodily elimination.

Each of our children is unique. Each has his own time to learn to be toilet trained. Most children can start somewhere between eighteen months and two years. Be sure that you as well as your child are ready for the experience.

I tell parents—especially mothers—that the key to potty training is to remain relaxed and calm. Don't get uptight and tense. Your child will sense your feelings and get uptight and tense right along with you.

My wife and I both remember the day she announced to one of our daughters, "This is the day you're going to be toilet trained." Sande had become tired of dirty diapers and had decided that the whole situation needed some "discipline." Of course, this approach to discipline met with total disaster. Our daughter sensed Sande's tension and responded appropriately. The entire operation was a total failure, despite my wife's use of a reward system which included giving our daughter some candy every time she got near or on the potty. Where did my wife learn about using candy as a reward? You guessed it. From a book written on toilet training by—you guessed it again—a psychologist!

After the first debacle everybody forgot about toilet training and relaxed for a few months. When our daughter was about two years old, my wife thought it was time to try again. This time she followed the advice of her *favorite* psy-

chologist (me). She bought a plastic training potty and simply left it in the bathroom. Our daughter "discovered" the
potty and started using it with great enthusiasm. In three
days she was totally trained. We did reinforce her learning
with a reward—some frilly underwear (for my daughter, not
my wife).

I always caution parents that when it comes to potty
training, children can exercise a great deal of control over
adults. They begin to feel a certain amount of power over
the big people who up until then have controlled their lives.
When you think about it, it's not too hard to understand
why a child gets these ideas of power. We really do act
rather silly and say some silly things after a child has gone
potty. Reinforce the child, yes; but to say, "Ohhhh, would
you look at that!" or "Look at the pretty present Festus gave
to Mommy," is really making far too much out of a basic
act.

Some parents try to train their children by using a con-
traption that fits on top of a full-size toilet. A far better approach is to get your child a potty chair, the kind that sits on
the floor and is the child's size. He can sit on it without any
fear of falling. If your first attempts fail and the child isn't
interested, you may want to just put the chair away for a
month, and then try later.

Or, you may want to take the approach that I prefer. I
think the best way to toilet train a child is to buy the little
potty chair, put it in the bathroom, and don't ever mention a
word about it. Let the child discover the potty chair for
himself. If he uses it appropriately, encourage him. Hold
him, talk to him, and communicate that he is really getting
big and learning to act grown-up.

Entire books have been written on how to toilet train
children. If you feel the need for more ideas on how to go
about it, contact your pediatrician. The major principle of
Reality Discipline that you want to use in toilet training is to
relax, be calm, and let nature take its course. There isn't a
more natural act in the entire world and your child will

learn when he or she is ready. Whatever you do, never be intimidated or fooled by claims from other mothers who have read some book about "toilet training in less than one hour." Believe me, that is *not* reality.

Selfishness

A definite reality of life is that our children are self-centered little creatures. Many times we are left shaking our heads, wondering why our kids can only think of themselves. The answer is simple. They are children and it is characteristic of a child to think only of himself. He has to learn how to think of others.

It is ironic that while one of the chief responsibilities of parents is to help their children learn how to think of others and not only of themselves, at the same time, a key error that many parents make is to focus on pleasing their children and making them happy. I'm not saying that we should try to make our children miserable. But I see case after case where parents are so busy making their children happy and trying to do what pleases them that any teaching they are trying to do about "thinking of others instead of yourself" is lost in the shuffle.

One typical example of how this happens is in the category of giving your children gifts. I do a lot of traveling and I am sympathetic toward parents who want to bring home gifts from their travels to give to the children. I have done it myself. But I also try to caution parents (myself included) to not *always* bring a treat home for a child. If this becomes a regular routine, the child views the gift as his right. People don't have a "right" to a gift. A gift is supposed to be an act of affection toward another person.

I recall a TV talk show interview. The host asked me what I thought he should do about his son. It seems that his nine-year-old often did not like the gifts the talk show host brought home from his travels. His boy was energetic, affectionate, and by all standards a "pretty good kid." But he soon turned his "dislike" for his father's gifts into a sort of game. Almost every time his father brought him a gift, he would carry on and complain. The father ended up feeling guilty and irritated because he had knocked himself out to bring home an appropriate gift, and the boy didn't like it.

I told the talk show host that the next time this happened he should proceed as follows: as soon as the boy expressed dislike or disdain for a gift, the father should simply say, "I'm sorry you don't like it. May I have it back, please? I'm sure you don't want to be bothered with it."

Then the father could take it and do one of several things. Perhaps a younger or older brother or sister might like the gift. Or perhaps a neighbor child would appreciate the gift. Whatever was done should be done swiftly and directly. If possible, the gift could even be returned where it was purchased.

I cautioned the father to do all of this calmly and with love. If the child sensed that the father was simply "getting revenge" or was simply venting hurt feelings, the discipline would be ineffective. What the father was trying to do, in this case, was simply communicate to his son, "Hey, I love you. I bring you gifts because I want to tell you how much I love you. If you don't like the gifts, then I don't imagine you want them cluttering up your room."

I made one other suggestion to the talk show host father. It is something I try to do myself. Parents should get out of the habit of bringing home gifts every time they travel. If a parent has to travel a great deal, he may use gifts as a bribe or a way of relieving his own guilt. But gifts should be a treat given once in a while, not every week, every month, or every trip. What we really want to teach children is that they should be happy that Daddy is back home. They should experience the joy of Daddy's homecoming and not necessarily the joy of receiving another gift.

Another means of combating self-centeredness in children is to start teaching them at an early age that it is truly more blessed to give than to receive. They should be encouraged to do things for other people whenever possible. For example, there might be an elderly couple in the neighborhood who could use some chores done, free of charge. If you really want to make this effective, make it a family project. Mom, Dad, and the kids can all go over and do some yard work for such a couple as an act of love. *Showing* your kids how to be unselfish is far more effective than *telling* them.

Sexual Exploration

Whenever I am speaking at a seminar and the topic of sex comes up, the crowd becomes notably more quiet. I think the reason for this is that, particularly in America, we have never become comfortable with speaking about sex. When I talk with mothers and fathers in my office, they often report that their children have discovered their genitalia and are "touching themselves," and what should they do?

My first piece of advice is to not panic. Children do, in fact, discover their genitalia almost immediately after birth and they continue to have a fascination with touching themselves.

But how are the parents supposed to talk to a child when this occurs? I believe the key is to convey to the child that it's very natural to want to touch your own body. At a very early age, give him or her guidelines that it's okay to touch yourself, but that you should not touch other people's bodies without their permission.

Of course, there are situations where other children do "give their permission." Kids are well known for playing house or doctor and "checking each other out." How is a parent to handle this? First of all, understand that the motivation for "playing doctor" usually stems from a child's need to determine if all boys and girls are built the same. About 95 percent of the men and women I work with in private practice admit to sexual exploration (playing doctor) with same-sex children when they were small.

If you do find your child or children playing doctor, the more calmly you react to such normal behavior, the better. Simply take your child aside and explain that his or her curiosity is very natural. However, caution your child that touching the bodies of others can create upsetting feelings. Tell your child you will talk with him or her about bodies and how they function. Tell him that you'll get a book that will "help us answer the questions we have."

I also recommend telling the other child or children's parents involved in the playing-doctor episode about the "clinic" you conducted with your own child, and briefly outline the course of action you plan to take.

And then follow through with what you said you would do. Get an appropriate book (a good one is *The Wonderful Story of How You Were Born* by Sidonie Gruenberg, published by Doubleday). Use the book as a springboard to further discussions.

I also highly recommend to parents that they share with their children about times they played doctor when they were young. I recommend this because such an admission reinforces in the child's mind that what he has done is natural and not something to feel guilty about. It also opens many avenues for further communication. The principle of Reality Discipline is that the parents must be willing to share the realities of their own experiences with their children in order to have honest and open communication.

Never punish a child for natural curiosity about his or her body. If you are overreactive and produce guilt and fear in your child, you may sow seeds in his mind that will sprout into abnormal sexual attitudes later in life.

Playing doctor is one problem, but what does a mother do when she finds her five-year-old daughter stimulating herself while sitting on the floor watching Saturday-morning cartoons? The key to any encounter with your children over the touching of their genitals is to be calm, warm, and positive. Never be critical, condemning, or hysterical. You do not want your children to associate their genitalia with something bad, evil, or dirty.

In every way possible, try to convey to your children at a very early age that all parts of their bodies are good, wonderful, and given by God. Everything we are is part of God's plan for our lives. As your children get older (above six) you can start talking about the gift of sex and how Mommy and Daddy make babies. I have already mentioned an excellent book by Sidonie Gruenberg. Another good one is *How to Teach Your Child About Sex* by Grace H. Ketterman, M.D., published by Fleming H. Revell Company.

Seminar audiences often ask me to share any experiences that my wife and I have had in this area with our own children and their exploration of the genitalia. The most humorous incident occurred one day while I was at the office. The phone rang and it was Sande, who was practically hysterical. She was crying and all I could get out of her was that something was wrong with Kevin, who was nineteen months old at the time. I immediately thought of our swimming pool in the backyard and thought the worst. Had she discovered him floating in the pool? No, that wasn't it.

"Well, then, what's wrong?" I asked. "Tell me, quick."

"Well," she said, "well, it's his thing."

"His thing?"

"Yes—you know, his *thing.*"

"Well, what's wrong with his thing?" I asked.

"It's purple!" she burst out.

"It's purple?" I echoed. "What do you mean, it's purple?"

Sande went on from there to explain that little Kevin had taken down his diapers, found a purple Magic Marker, and had done some rather creative artwork on his "thing." Then he came marching out into the family room like Napoleon to show my wife.

At this point I broke up laughing. I shouldn't have laughed, but I couldn't help it.

"Well, why are you laughing?" Sande asked.

I could tell she wasn't too happy with my amusement.

"Well, honey," I replied. "Little boys do things like that—you shouldn't worry."

Sande was incredulous. "They *do?*" she said. "Do you think it's *really* okay?"

"At nineteen months, it's okay," I assured her. "I just hope he doesn't get a rash."

And so, that was the day my wife learned that little boys do many "funny little things like that." The point of the story is that children are going to experiment—with themselves and sometimes with one another. Reality Discipline demands that you keep your cool and never communicate to the child that his honest curiosity is dirty or perverted. At the same time, always stress the private nature of the sexual organs and that God gave us our sex organs as part of His wonderful plan for our lives.

Sibling Rivalry

Few families with more than one child escape problems with sibling rivalry. I believe that part of the problem arises from the tendency for parents to feel that all children have to be treated the same. At least you can be sure that's what the children try to convey. What one child gets, the other child wants.

My own children tried to work me along these lines on different occasions. Holly would say, "Daddy, how come she got that and I didn't get that? How come Krissy can do that and I can't?"

Sometimes I would tease Holly a little and "pull the rug" by saying something outlandish like, "Well, obviously it's because your mother and I love her so much more than we love you!"

If Holly continued to pester me and demand equal treatment, I would finally challenge her with something like this:

"Okay Holly, if you really want me to treat you exactly like your little sister, Krissy, your bedtime is now 8:30 instead of 9:00 P.M. and your allowance is two dollars and fifty cents instead of three dollars."

At this point, Holly would decide she really didn't want to be treated the same in all circumstances. The above illustration worked quite nicely for me because in that case Holly was older than Krissy and already was receiving more privileges, such as a later bedtime and a larger allowance. We had allowed Krissy to do something that Holly thought she could do, too, and that is what caused the problem. But what happens if a younger child wants the same privileges that his older brother or sister is getting? The principle of Reality Discipline to always invoke is that you love all your children equally but you treat them differently, according to what you believe is appropriate and fair at the time.

One of the major forces behind sibling rivalry is that our kids want the best of both worlds. They want to be sure that brother or sister doesn't get more than they do, but at the same time they want to be treated differently—as someone special. It's too easy for parents to fall into the trap of having to play judge and jury.

Much of what I mentioned under "Fighting" applies to sibling rivalry. As I said in that section, you cannot fully eliminate rivalry between siblings; you should try to find ways to minimize and control it. In fact, allowing a child to vent frustrations and feelings about a sibling is healthy and will in the long run defuse hostility, anger, and chronic rivalry.

Obviously, the trick is to keep it under control and not let it get out of hand. The basic principle of Reality Discipline to use with sibling rivalry is to always try to get your children to work out situations and disagreements among themselves if at all possible. For example, if two children, seven and nine years old, are having a hassle, remove them from the family room and put them in a room alone with instructions to stay in there until they can work things out.

Always remember that much of the verbal clawing that goes on among siblings is for the benefit of their parents. They want us to intervene and get involved. One child takes a cheap shot at his brother or sister and gets a derogatory response in return and before you know it, the whole family is in the middle of a war. If kids want to be miserable, if they want to yell and scream at each other, they can do it outside of the house or in some room at the other end of the house. They are not to do it at the dinner table or in the family room.

Another key Reality Discipline principle to remember is that children will consciously or unconsciously lay traps for their parents to attempt to get them into their arguments and disagreements and involve their parents in solving the problem. The responsible parent, however, uses Reality Discipline to stand back and allow the children to work out their own difficulties, if at all possible.

In traditional homes where reward and punishment are the rule, children often try to set each other up. They want the parents to intervene and pass down some kind of judgment in order to punish a brother or sister. This kind of "judge and jury" game usually has a 50 percent accuracy rate at best and usually creates more chaos and ill will than it solves.

In my counseling practice, I've heard many youngest-child reports about how they enjoyed setting up an older sibling and pushing the right buttons to get older brother or sister to hit them. Then, with perfect timing and theatrical skills worthy of an Academy Award, this youngest child would scream, whine, or yell in such a way to make the parent believe that death was imminent. Usually, the parent's reaction was to punish the older brother or sister swiftly and aggressively. Although the younger child had to bear the pain of getting a hit a few times by the older brother or sister, he always felt it was worth it. Why? Because he truly enjoyed watching the parent wale the older brother or sister.

We psychologists frequently counsel family situations where we see the oldest child going through life seemingly "looking over his shoulder" at the siblings who are closing in behind. The technical word for this is *dethronement*. The dethronement problem is always more pronounced when siblings are close in age, and it is heightened when siblings are of the same sex.

While it may not be perfect in every situation, I still believe that the best system to insure individual and fair treatment of children is to "grant the birthright" to the eldest child. This means the eldest child has more freedom and privileges, but he or she also has more responsibilities.

Swearing

One day my six-year-old suddenly turned the air blue with a four-letter word. Her mother looked at me and I looked at her. Then we both looked at our daughter. Without a word, I picked her up, took her to her bedroom, and sat her on the bed. Then I let fly with several choice words that would made a sailor's ears turn green. My six-year-old was shocked. Her eyes were like Ping-Pong balls. I looked her right in those Ping-Pong-ball-sized eyes and said, "Krissy, Daddy and Mommy know every filthy and dirty word in the book. But we have made some choices as Christians not to use those words."

Of course, Krissy was in tears by now and very sorry for what she had said. We assured her that we forgave her and then we made a point to talk with her about the fact that she was going to hear that kind of word in school and on the playground. She would see filthy words written on rest room walls and she was going to hear adults use them as well. This is the reality of the situation. As much as we hate to see it, our children are exposed to ugly, filthy, profane words early in their lives and it continues throughout life.

I believe that the key approach when you hear your child swearing or talking obscenely is to let the child know that you know all the words—every one of them—but you have chosen not to use them. Tell the child specifically why you have chosen not to use these words. If the words include taking God's name in vain, explain that the Bible clearly teaches us to not take God's name in vain and that we love God far too much to do that anyway. As for obscenities and dirty expressions, explain to your child that in your home you choose not to use that kind of language because it is crude, ignorant, and disrespectful for all concerned.

The above approach is infinitely better than traditional punitive measures such as a slap in the face, a spanking, or the classic "washing the child's mouth out with soap." All of these may relieve your tensions and anger, but they will have nothing to do with discipline or training.

Talking Back

Unless you are running your home with the authoritarian precision of a dictator, your children probably feel free to talk back to you on occasion. Many parents I deal with have a real problem when their children "smart mouth" them. They want their children to be able to challenge them and to say how they feel, but when they cross that unseen but very real line and become impudent, a little switch goes off inside a parent's brain. A little voice says, *You can't say that to me. Don't you know who I am? I'm your mother!*

Sometimes the parent feeds that exact message right back to the child and, of course, this can lead to more talking back and more impudence.

When your child becomes powerful with you, you should not become powerful in return. All you do by trying to exert your power is to lay the foundation for a good knock-down-drag-out battle. There are any number of ways to handle talking back.

If you have trouble keeping your temper, you might try

leaving the room for a minute or two. This conveys to the child, "I choose not to fight with you." A short trip to your bedroom perhaps, and turning the radio on (to drown out the back talk if necessary) can allow you to stay in control of your emotions. A caution here, however, is to only be gone a couple of minutes. You do not want the child to get the idea that he can "drive Mommy out" any time he wants. And once you have gotten control, you must go back and deal with the situation.

One way to deal with smart talk is to simply send the child an "I" message that says you do not appreciate this kind of behavior and will not tolerate it. If he chooses to continue this kind of talk, he will be the one who is removed from the scene and isolated for a brief time if necessary.

If a child persists in talking back, he may be asking for a swat. If the child is seven years old or under, a swat may well be in order. Just be sure that you are in control of your emotions and that after the swat you let the child know he is loved but he cannot talk that way to his parents.

Suppose the "talking back" is centered around what little Zelda is going to have to wear to a birthday party. If Zelda gets very vocal and abusive in protesting what she has to wear, you can "pull the rug" by simply announcing, "I guess you are not going to the party."

Whatever parents do, I insist that they never accept smart-mouth behavior. Furthermore, it is essential for women not to take any guff from their sons as well as for dads to not take any guff from their daughters. There is a very powerful relationship between a mother and her son and a dad and his daughter. What parents are really doing is training their children to learn who they are as male and female and what being a man or woman is all about. It is particularly important for mothers not to train their sons to believe that they can walk all over women.

Psychological research continues to demonstrate that men tend to marry women who have personality traits similar to their mothers, and women tend to marry men with personalities similar to their fathers. This kind of research evidence only underlines the need for parents to be aware of the "specialness" of mother-son, father-daughter relationships. When parents stand their ground with opposite-sex children, they are actually teaching a great deal about respect and love in a marriage relationship. It may not be evident at the moment, but when Mom refuses to let little Buford get away with smart talk, and when Dad brings little Zelda up short for a fit of temper, they are actually increasing their children's chances for ultimate marital happiness in the future.

A key concept with which Reality Discipline agrees completely is: "God didn't create any of us to be walked on!"

Tattling

One of the oldest and most potent tricks children use to needlessly drag parents into their hassles is tattling on one another. The problem with allowing tattling to ever start is that once you hear one tale, you are going to have to listen to all of them. I suggest to parents that they never listen to anything that sounds like tattling. Of course, the parent must be able to differentiate between the kind of talebearing that is designed to simply get a brother or sister in trouble and a report of something of a more serious nature. For example, if a twelve-year-old brother is beating up on an eight-year-old sister, the sister should have some kind of recourse to let Mom know she is getting worked over. But in many cases, children will come with their little stories about what big brother is doing or about what sister did, and so on.

When you can detect that no real harm is being done, just make a direct statement such as, "Honey, I'm sure you can handle it. You and your sister work it out." Make this kind of encouraging statement, which tells your child that you are not going to give in and be used or manipulated. Again, let me emphasize that there are times when a child may have a bona fide complaint. But if you can detect that he or she is simply trying to manipulate you to get his own way, you must act quickly to put a stop to it. Otherwise, you walk directly into the trap. You will be running around in circles as each child yanks you on the end of his own little chain to get you involved.

When you allow the child to jerk you around like this, you inevitably have to play the old judge-and-jury game in which you have to make a decision based upon very limited and biased information which has been given to you by one or both of your children. Reality Discipline does not work well when you have to play judge and jury. You want reality to be the teacher and the judge if judgment is necessary. Whenever possible, stay out of the hassles and disagreements that your children get into and let them be accountable for their own actions. When necessary, you may have to step in, but these times should be kept at a minimum.

I know of one mother who tried to keep tattling in proper perspective this way: when any of her three children came with his tale of woe, she would listen carefully. If it was a simple "Brian hit me" or "Vicki won't let me play" tale, the mother would respond, "Thank you," and nothing was done. But if it was a genuine report of real abuse or mayhem which often involved two against one, with that one child in drastic trouble, then she would respond with appropriate action. Her children soon learned that when they just tattled they were usually ignored, and so they stopped giving those kinds of reports and just made the more genuine complaints.

The TV Monster

Television is a growing problem for Christian parents today. The channels are full of garbage that ranges from violence and immoral sex to just plain poor programming and poor taste. But while TV is a problem, it also presents an opportunity for using Reality Discipline effectively. Here are some steps that you should take.

1. *Construct guidelines for watching television in your fam-*

ily. Find out what your kids want to watch and view some of these programs yourself. If some of them are not acceptable, tell your children what your feelings are and explain why you feel the way you do.

The term *acceptable* is extremely subjective. The important thing is that you come up with basic guidelines for what is acceptable TV in your home, and then stick with those guidelines.

2. *Another important factor is to limit the time your children spend watching television.* Always stress the Reality Discipline idea that work still comes before play and homework is done before TV is even an option.

3. *Monitor your children's program selection even if you can't always be there.* Devices are already being marketed that allow the parent to preselect television programming for as much as a week at a time. This kind of gadget is especially helpful in single-parent homes where children have to be by themselves for longer periods of time.

4. *Do some homework with the* TV Guide *each week.* Identify TV programs or specials that are worthwhile for the entire family. Make it a big event. Pop a little corn and enjoy it together.

5. *Make yourself more acquainted with cable television and what it offers.* Today, twenty-four-hour Christian programming is a reality in many areas, especially those serviced by cable television. Networks such as CBN, PTL, and TBN are all providing Christian families with much greater options for television viewing.

Time Out

By "time out" I am talking about stopping what the child is doing and making him sit down for a while—on a chair or in his room—to do some thinking.

Parents often ask me if time out is a good thing. Is it a good way to administer discipline? I always tell them that indeed it is. There are many moments through the day when Mom or Dad needs to call time out. For the benefit of the social order in the home, little Festus or Felicia needs to sit down on a chair, or go sit in his or her room and do some thinking and quieting down.

When you call time out on one of your children, you are simply telling him or her, "Your behavior is so obnoxious that you have earned the right to stay away from the rest of the family for a period of time."

When I talk about time out, I always add a word of caution. Whenever you isolate a child, don't overdo it. (Four months *is* too long, although I realize there are times when it is tempting.) Five to ten minutes is usually plenty of time for children six years old and above. Around two minutes is sufficient for preschoolers.

Keep in mind that time out is not a punishment but simply a method of helping your child understand he is responsible for his actions. When his actions become unacceptable, he has to stop and realize what he has been doing. If the child's behavior improves after time out, fine. But if he goes right back to doing the same thing that caused the original disruption or problem, you may have to call time out again.

Each time you find time out necessary, it's important to have a brief bit of communication with the child. Ask little Felicia, "How do you feel now? Are you ready to come back and play by the rules? We really want you back with the rest of the family—if you're ready."

While doing this communicating, always be sure that you touch your child. Give hugs and loves as you explain why the child was isolated and why that behavior is not acceptable.

Traveling Terrors

Suppose you are planning to travel across country on your annual two-week vacation. Regarding your children, you can: a) leave them home; b) send them to camp; c) take them along; d) send them ahead UPS. If the answer is c (take them along), you probably already know that traveling with children is difficult.

One surefire way to get there without problems is to carry them "deer style" on the front of the car. If you are old enough to remember that cars used to have fenders, perhaps you can picture little Buford and Festus strapped up there above the headlights, guaranteeing you will arrive without any fighting, bickering, or forty-seven pit stops. But since you probably don't have the fenders or the heart for such a radical solution, I suggest you keep the following basics in mind as you travel with your children:

1. *If you have young children (five years old and under), tape record all of their favorite stories.* They can spend hours listening and while you may get a little bored by endless reruns of Dr. Seuss or Baby Moses, it is infinitely better than listening to bickering and whining. Also, bring along a blank tape or two and let your kids do some recording of their own. They love to hear the sound of their own voices.

2. *Kids frequently ask for something to eat or drink.* A wise parent brings along some popcorn. It's great roughage for kids. It does make a mess, but it is easy to vacuum up later. Popcorn is much better than chocolate bars. It's healthier and won't stain (as long as you go easy on the butter).

Also take along something nutritious to drink. Kids get enough sugar poured into their bodies. Diet drinks are as bad or worse because of the chemicals. Little cans of apple or pineapple juice are perfect.

3. *Many parents are aware of standard traveling games like counting telephone poles, cows, and so on.* Another old standby is finding license plates from other states. Another excellent "pass the time" gimmick is a "grab bag" or oatmeal box containing *washable, nontoxic* markers and some pads of paper. *Do not bring crayons.* They will melt in the sun and cause disaster in cars.

Another good product to bring along, especially for kids under five years old, is Colorforms—little plastic cutout figures that adhere to the car windows. They are ideal for use in cars and even on trains and planes because they are easily removed later. Kids can amuse themselves for hours with Big Bird, Yogi Bear, and dozens of other familiar cartoon characters.

4. *The "I need to go potty" cry is bound to be heard—usually every few miles.* One way to keep the potty cry down to a minimum is this: every time you stop, for any reason, take the child to look at the rest room. Kids are fascinated by rest rooms. They love to just look them over, whether they want to use them or not. And one out of two times they probably will want to use them. All of this helps eliminate some of the pit stops that parents often find themselves making.

5. *Avoid making promises while traveling.* Don't promise your children anything. There is no reason to do so and it can get you in all kinds of difficulties. Promising them it won't rain, or that "we will be there by noon," can give you figurative and literal headaches. Kids have memories like elephants and you don't need mile after mile of, "But you promised. . . ."

6. *Don't spit on your children.* I know that sounds a little off the wall, but I am serious. Many parents find themselves in situations where they need to get the children cleaned up. Because they have nothing handy they use their own saliva, with a hankie, to clean off Buford's face. If there is any horrifying memory I have of my own childhood, it is having Mommy's saliva all over my face.

Instead of spitting on your kids, take a Tupperware or other container full of wet washcloths or buy packages of Wet Ones.

The name of all of the above games is "diversionary tactics." It is frustrating (maddening as the day wears on) to have children crawling all over themselves and you and demanding Mommy's and Daddy's attention. All of the above ideas are designed to help children amuse themselves and give their parents a break. With a little preplanning and preparation, you can make that trip across country with the kids far more pleasant—for you and for them.

A Final Word

In the foregoing pages I have sought to give you the foundational principles of Reality Discipline, along with as many practical suggestions as possible for use in situations you face daily in your own family. I realize I have not covered everything. The problems in parenting are virtually limitless. What I have tried to do, however, is to touch on those major areas where parents frequently ask me for help.

Most important, I have tried to give you a basic strategy for parenting that you can modify and adapt to fit your own personality. You may not use exactly the same actions that I have suggested in every case. What is important, however, is that you do *act*—quickly and decisively—to teach your child the reality of being accountable for what he or she does.

One of the most tragic news stories I ever read was head-lined, "Injured Boy Wins $810,000 Suit." The item told of how a twelve-year-old had lost part of his left foot while trying to hitch a ride on a slow-moving freight train. In handing down the $810,000 settlement the judge ruled that the boy was to start receiving monthly payments at the age eighteen, which would continue for life. The attorney representing the lad based his argument on the charge of negligence against the city because officials knew there was a hole in the fence along the railroad tracks and *they should have known children would be tempted to go through it.*

This story is tragic for two reasons: first, a young boy was crippled for life, but even more tragic is the fact that the courts ruled in favor of irresponsibility. At age twelve a child should be able to make a much wiser decision than to climb through a fence and try to hop a freight train. The same irony is seen in an advertisement you may have observed in a newspaper or on television. The ad states, "Don't make a kid go wrong!" The message admonishes motorists to not leave their keys in their cars because this will tempt youngsters to steal them! Is there any doubt that the time has come for Reality Discipline?

I'm not saying that using Reality Discipline gives you an ironclad guarantee that you will never have problems or that your children will never misbehave in a serious way. Reality Discipline does not even guarantee that your children will become Christians. But as you use the game plan and strategies that are basic to Reality Discipline, you will be training your children by relying on actions, not words, to help them learn to be accountable and responsible for their decisions.

Decision making—particularly the important decisions—is much harder for the child who has been allowed to run free and "do his own thing." It is equally hard for the child who has been under an authoritarian yoke where all of his decisions were made for him. But the child reared through Reality Discipline has had the opportunity to see what *loving authority* is all about.

I know what you may be thinking: *That sounds like a nice theory, Dr. Leman. If I had a degree in psychology I might be able to pull it off.*

Believe me, I—the so-called expert—know how difficult it can be. Kids test us constantly and we don't always pass with flying colors. I still remember an incident when Holly was well into her "terrible twos." She got into a particularly bad mood and totally defied me. Finally, I had to pick her up, put her in her room, and say, "Holly, you have to stay in here until you settle down and can behave yourself."

According to my advice to other parents (see page 178), Holly was supposed to sit quietly for a few minutes, realize she had to be responsible for her actions, and then rejoin the family group in a much better mood. It didn't happen quite that way. In thirty seconds my tiny daughter was out of her room and right back at me, doing her best to make life less than serene. I redeposited her in her room with the same admonition: "Holly, I wish you could come back and be with Mommy and me, but you are just not ready."

I went out and closed the door, quite sure that this time Holly would get the message. But Holly was not in a message-receiving mood. This time it took *less* than thirty seconds for her to come through the door and start biting my ankles again.

The situation was becoming a bit desperate. I had already tried a swat in the proper area, but Holly's rage only increased. I decided to resort to my ultimate weapon: the Kevin Leman Memorial Doorknob. This is an ingenious invention of my own making that is simply an ordinary doorknob that has been reversed to lock on the outside. I should have used it the first time I put Holly in her room, but I had wrongly assumed that I could talk her into cooperating. With a quick flip of the lock button Holly was secure, or so I thought.

Predictably, Holly pleaded, wailed, screamed, and gave the general impression she was on a medieval torture rack. It only lasted a minute or so and then she was quiet. As I was congratulating myself for being courageous enough to use "loving authority," the doorbell rang. As fate would have it, my mother had dropped by for an unexpected visit, and she especially wanted to see Holly!

Grandma greeted me and immediately asked where her "little princess" was. I furtively glanced toward Holly's bedroom door and then almost gasped with dismay. From under the door crept tiny white fingers that mutely semaphored a plea for rescue. Grandma's keen eye instantly spotted Holly's hand, outlined on the bright-blue rug. She fixed me with a withering gaze and demanded: "You didn't lock my granddaughter in her room, did you?"

"I sure did, Mom."

Grandma gave a disgusted snort. "You, you *psychologist*, you!" was all she could manage, and she stalked away.

I stood there, staring at Holly's little fingers as they continued to send their "Mayday" message to all the world. I couldn't see her face, but I pictured her lying on her stomach, her "blankie" tucked under her arm and a smug little smile on her cherub face. I had won the battle, but I wasn't sure about the war. I waited a few more minutes and then opened the door.

"Are you ready to come out now and be part of the family?" I asked.

My two-and-a-half-year-old gave a brief nod and almost strutted past me to go find her grandma, who was sitting in the living room muttering about psychologists and what she had done to deserve a son who had become one.

When I happened to walk by a few minutes later, there was Holly, snuggled on Grandma's lap. I tried to greet them amiably, but they both gave me looks of cool disdain. I spent the rest of the day not feeling all that loving, or as if I had much authority!

I tell you that story to underscore one important point: when rearing children you will know many moments of reality when things don't go exactly by the book, whether it be this book or one written by some other child-rearing expert. My encounter with Holly and Grandma left me feeling like anything but the capable professional who handles every family crisis with fluid precision. It would be several more years before Holly would write me that precious note that I shared with you in chapter 1 (page 31). Then she would say:

My father is the gratist, for your the best, caring, Loveing, THE BEST!!!!!!

And why would she say I was the best? The last line of her note contains the secret:

even when you disaplin me, I Love you the same.

Holly didn't understand parental strategy and theories, but she could understand being disciplined with love. I have written this book to help you discipline with love as effectively as you can. You don't have to be perfect. There will be many times when you will feel frustrated and baffled. There will be times when your children or your spouse (or maybe Grandma) will send you on a guilt trip or running for cover to hide your embarrassment.

Those are the moments when you need *the courage to be imperfect,* just as I did when those tiny fingers crept out from under the door. In those moments you never give up. You stick to your game plan, always remembering that parenting is a *very* long game and one strikeout or fumble does not decide the outcome. What will decide the outcome is your commitment to train your children to be responsible and accountable for their decisions: "the loving discipline the Lord himself approves."

Publications by Dr. Kevin Leman

A Child's Ten Commandments to Parents
Parenthood Without Hassles—Well, Almost
Sex Begins in the Kitchen
Smart Girls Don't, and Guys Don't Either

Other Family and Child-Rearing Resources by Dr. Kevin Leman

Video Series

Growing Up Whole in a Breaking Up World
Love 'Em and Keep 'Em: The Challenge of Raising Kids
Sex and the Christian Family

Video series available for rental/purchase from

Covenant Video
3200 W. Foster Avenue
Chicago, Illinois 60625
1-800-621-1290

Film Series
Growing Up Whole in a Breaking Down World

Film series distributed by

Gospel Films
Box 455
Muskegon, Michigan 49443
1-800-253-0413

For information regarding speaking engagements or seminars, write or call:

Dr. Kevin Leman
1161 North El Dorado Place
Suite 213
Tucson, Arizona 85715
602-886-9925